Starting &
Running a
Greeting
Cards
Business

Lots of **practical advice**
to help you build an **exciting**
and **profitable** business

 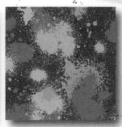  

Elizabeth White

howtobooks

Published by How To Books Ltd,
Spring Hill House, Spring Hill Road,
Begbroke, Oxford OX5 1RX, United Kingdom.
Tel: (01865) 375794. Fax: (01865) 379162.
info@howtobooks.co.uk
www.howtobooks.co.uk

How To Books greatly reduce the carbon footprint of their books by sourcing their
typesetting and printing in the UK.

British Library Cataloguing in Publication Data
A catalogue record for this book is available from the British Library

ISBN 978 1 84528 264 6

Cover design by Baseline Arts Ltd, Oxford
Produced for How To Books by Deer Park Productions, Tavistock, Devon
Typeset by TW Typesetting, Plymouth, Devon
Printed and bound by Cromwell Press, Trowbridge, Wiltshire

NOTE: The material contained in this book is set out in good faith for general
guidance and no liability can be accepted for loss or expense incurred as a result of
relying in particular circumstances on statements made in the book. The laws and
regulations are complex and liable to change, and readers should check the current
position with the relevant authorities before making personal arrangements.

Contents

Acknowledgements

Many people have supported, encouraged and helped me with the preparation of this book. I would particularly like to thank the following Rachel Hare, Belly Button Designs, Chris Griffiths of A La Carte Business Services Ltd., Joe Sheldon of Teamprint, Hillside Printing Services, Angie and Paul Boyer at Craft & Design, Terry Osborn of nexus Solicitors, Isobel Martinson of the Giftware Association, staff at the Greeting Card Association and colleagues at Bolton Business Ventures. I am grateful to Nikki Read and her team at How to Books for their encouragement and professionalism.

And a special thank you to all the cardmakers and artists who inspired me to write this book. I wish you all success in your business ventures.

For Emily

Preface

If you are a creative person then making and selling greeting cards is a great way to start a business. The majority of UK consumers buy at least one card a year, and many buy a lot more. Birthday cards remain the most popular with peak sales for other cards at Christmas, Mother's Day, and Valentine's Day. The market is growing all the time, however, and cards are available for numerous occasions. New reasons to celebrate seem to be discovered all the time. Civil Partnership cards have recently come on to the market and there are even cards to congratulate you on your divorce. Making and selling cards is one of the most popular ways of starting a small business.

> ◆ KEY ◆
>
> It is the type of business that can be started at the kitchen table and end up in the global market.

Making cards is also an excellent way for artists and makers to increase their income as they can sell cards alongside their main product. It is also a good way for artists to promote their work – people cannot always afford an original painting but by buying a card they can buy an image of your work.

There are various ways of starting a card business. Many people begin by making cards at home using materials from art and craft shops. When their cards start selling to family and friends they begin to wonder if they have a potential business. Other people plunge straight in the deep end by designing a range and having the cards printed.

> **♦ KEY ♦**
>
> However you decide to start you will soon become addicted to what is a very exciting and interesting business to run.

Before deciding which direction to go in, spend some time in all types of card shops, at markets and fairs. Buy some of the cards, take them home, and compare the quality of the card and the envelope with the price. Identify what type of card they are – for example handmade, hand-assembled or printed.

> **♦ TIP ♦**
>
> The more research you do the better your chance of success.

Small-scale greeting card makers often specialise in handmade cards. These can be created using materials such as flowers, beads, glitter, wire and fabric, or by using a computer package to design and print the cards. Another popular way of producing cards is to use your own artwork, whether it is cartoons or watercolour landscapes.

> **♦ KEY ♦**
>
> The possibilities for creating card designs are endless.

Deciding to start a business can be an exciting challenge. There are many large card companies that started life on the kitchen table. As the business grows, decisions will have to be made as to how you are going to operate. It's not uncommon for handmade card companies to receive an order for 500 identical cards; this can be quite challenging – but where there is a problem there is always a solution.

> **♦ KEY ♦**
>
> It can be very exciting seeing cards that you have made or designed on sale in the shops.

Running a business also means that you will not be focused solely on creating the cards. You will also need to take care of finding suppliers, production, financing, marketing, selling, bookkeeping and all the administrative tasks. If you are not happy to take all that on board then you could consider setting up as a designer where you can concentrate on the creative side of the business.

This book will guide you through all the stages of starting and running a successful Greeting Cards Business. It will help you avoid the pitfalls and will share with you the secrets of successful card companies. It is packed with information to help you succeed and build a successful greeting cards business.

1

What type of card business?

There are three main ways of starting a greeting cards business:

◆ Making and selling handmade cards

◆ Designing and printing cards

◆ Designing cards for a manufacturer

Choosing the right one for you will depend on your skills and experience, amount of capital available and personal preference.

Whether you decide to find a publisher, publish your own, make handmade cards or even open a shop, you will need to understand the way the greeting cards industry works. If you don't do your homework and study the business from all angles you risk getting lost in what is a fast-moving, exciting and challenging industry.

FINDING YOUR MARKET

There are hundreds of different types of greeting cards; it is important to decide what type of card you intend to produce or sell before setting up in business. This will help you identify the market for the cards and decide on pricing and where you will sell them. If you can think of a new idea to bring to the industry then you can make serious money. Be warned – the industry is addictive and once you start you will get hooked.

You can produce designs on the computer or use objects to create patterns and designs.

WHAT SKILLS DO YOU NEED TO RUN A GREETING CARDS BUSINESS?

Creativity

Creativity is a vital part of producing a card range. There is little point in copying someone else's cards. If you intend to produce original cards then you should try to produce something different. This will increase your chances of success. The ability to create saleable designs in whatever medium you choose is very important, as is originality which will make you stand out from the crowd.

If you lack creativity then you will need to employ a designer. If you want to supply ideas to the larger publishers then you will need to be able to draw, but if you are producing handmade cards this won't be necessary.

Money management

In addition to your creative skills it helps if you are good at controlling costs; wastage can be expensive in such a low value product. Running any business demands good money management, but if you can operate a household budget then you should be fine.

Another important factor is the amount of money you have available. You can start a business with very little capital by making handmade cards in the spare room and selling at craft fairs. On the other hand having ranges of cards printed and employing agents to sell them is a much more expensive option.

Selling skills

There are many ways to sell cards:

◆ friends and family

◆ the workplace

◆ craft fairs

◆ direct to shops

◆ trade fairs

◆ using agents

◆ by placing spinners in places such as hospitals.

If you are good at selling you may want to market them yourself. If not, you might need to employ an agent on your behalf.

IT skills

The ability to use computers is vital when running a business. You may need a website to promote your cards or you may wish to sell over the internet. Finding suppliers and potential customers is also easier with the internet. And many cards are designed using computer programs.

Administrative skills

There is inevitably a lot of paperwork involved in running any sort of business: keeping books, orders, invoices and general paperwork. Most creative people don't enjoy this part of the business but it is essential if you are to keep in control.

◆ TIP ◆

Don't worry if you don't have all these skills at the moment: you can learn them. There are numerous courses available for the creative and the business side.

Using your talents

If writing is your forte then you could sell verses to card manufacturers. If you have a talent for painting, photography, calligraphy and writing then you may want to use it in the business; if you don't want to make and sell the cards yourself then consider setting up as a card designer.

There is a huge demand for card designs from the larger card companies. Although individual design fees may not provide a large income, cards are generally produced in ranges which can increase your income.

◆ KEY ◆

It is very satisfying to walk into a shop and see your work on display and watch people admiring and purchasing your cards.

TYPES OF CARD

Artists' cards

These cards are generally produced by artists who want to earn extra money when selling at art fairs, or who want to produce something affordable for their customers to buy. Many of these will be bought for framing and as such they will command a higher price. They will also be original work, which again will add to their value. Despite the fact that they will be unique and command a premium price you will still have to be careful if you are to make a profit.

◆ TIP ◆

Make the cards the right size for standard frames and you will increase your sales.

Hand-painted cards

Hand-painting cards can be very time-consuming. To make it cost effective you need to find a method of painting cards which will take a minimum amount of time, such as painting 10 similar cards at once or painting all the skies in one go.

Some artists create lovely cards from paintings that haven't sold or have some areas of a painting which are better than others. This is fine if you have a market for one-off cards but if you are trying to produce a range it's unlikely to work.

Tips for hand-painted cards

Work on watercolour paper or card and then glue the result to the card base; this prevents expensive wastage if you make mistakes.

Clearly label the cards as original work; some artists label them 'frame or send' as many people will buy them to frame as pictures.

Handmade cards

The majority of cards made by craft workers fall into this category; they have a strong element of design and some artistic input making them difficult to copy. Customers will not buy cards which look amateurish or use cheap materials. Make sure you are producing the best cards you can using quality materials if you want to sell them commercially.

You can buy a huge range of items to stick on the cards to enhance your design but be careful as they often make the cards look amateurish. Lettering is important on handmade cards and if this is one of your weaknesses consider going on a calligraphy course or having the greetings printed.

◆ TIP ◆

If you are planning to produce these cards in quantity then you may have to employ someone else to help you make them. In this case you need to ensure that the skills needed to produce the card can be taught fairly easily.

Assembled cards

These cards are often mistaken for handmade by customers, but in fact are generally termed 'hand-assembled' by the trade. The cards consist of different shapes, stuck-on letters or other items assembled on the card. Although there is an element of creativity needed to design them, little skill is needed to assemble them.

Their advantage is that it is easy to produce a professional looking card; the disadvantage is that if it is easy for you it is easy for everyone else and your cards may not be unusual enough to find a market.

◆ TIP ◆

Although they can be a good product to sell at craft fairs, shops will probably find that there is not the level of design or artistic input required to make them worth stocking.

Stamped cards

Stamping is a very popular pastime and many people use it to make cards, as it is quick and easy to do. Selling these types of cards, however, is difficult. Because it is so quick and easy many people make them for their own use.

Stamps can be expensive, and if you are not careful you can spend a lot of money on them and never use them. If you like stamping, one way to make your range unusual is to experiment with different paints, inks and powders (especially metallic finishes) to create something special.

◆ TIP ◆

Stamping combined with other skills such as drawing can produce interesting and quality cards.

Hand-finished cards

This term applies to cards which are printed, and then have something extra added to make them into a semi-handmade card. This can be something attached with adhesive, like dried flowers, or a logo which is individually painted.

◆ TIP ◆

If you aim to produce cards in quantity to sell to shops, hand finished may be a good option. It is not as labour intensive as handmade but commands a higher price than printed cards.

Printed cards

To produce a range of printed cards you will need a substantial amount of capital. Retailers will want a large enough range to display properly and new designs at regular intervals. You need to be prepared to have enough money to allow you to build up regular stockists and a good portfolio of designs. You will also need to find a printer who is sympathetic and preferably who will let you experiment with different types of board. Remember the same design can look completely different on different boards.

◆ TIP ◆

The greeting-cards industry is very fast moving – a card has an average lifespan of only eight months. If your cards are successful you will have to constantly design and produce new ranges to keep up with the demand from shops.

You do not have to have a lot of cards professionally printed; at first you could print them using the computer to test the market. This will enable you to try out your designs without committing to huge printing costs.

Photographic cards

Selling cards featuring photographs either printed directly onto the cards, or actual photographs attached with glue, is a popular way for photographers to earn extra income. With modern camera equipment it's not difficult to produce technically good photographs – but creativity is important.

Knowing which market to target will help; photographs of local beauty spots will probably sell well at tourist information centres, floral photographs at garden centres, and so on.

◆ TIP ◆

If you have a hobby or special interest then consider this market. One photographer I know makes a good living producing cards and prints of lambrettas!

Commissioned cards

These are cards commissioned from you by customers. They could be for weddings, or other celebrations. To reach this market you will generally have to use different methods from the cards outlined above to obtain orders and market your cards. If you are specialising in weddings then you will need to take a stand at wedding fairs and build relationships with wedding planners and bridal shops. Advertising in bridal magazines is expensive but targets your market directly.

A website and good quality marketing material are essential as the market is for quality products and is not price sensitive. In fact orders can be very lucrative for a wedding – not only invitations but orders of service, place cards and menus can all add up to a substantial order.

Special events include:

◆ weddings

◆ business launches/events

◆ civil partnerships

◆ 18th and 21st birthdays

◆ wedding anniversaries.

One challenge when producing specially commissioned cards is to accommodate the customer's wishes. For instance a wedding might be themed and the cards will have to fit in with this. Sometimes this can be quite easy – for instance Art Deco or a gothic wedding. On other occasions the bride's ideas might be vague or there might be a 'committee' of people trying to influence the designs.

Civil partnerships are now very popular and can be a good market to target, particularly if you have connections in this area. Visit clubs and bars which cater for the gay market and leave your business cards and fliers.

◆ KEY ◆

There is also some demand for individual cards made especially for one person; these are particularly popular for new babies and Christenings. This type of business can be built up over the internet or by handing out fliers at craft fairs.

Internet cards

There have been many attempts to sell cards over the internet, but most of these have been unsuccessful. Cards appear to be a product that people like to choose themselves from shops. Some card companies, however, are now experiencing growth – one of these is www.moonpig.com. They specialise in personalising cards, which gives them an advantage over the shops. You can have a comic card with the name of the person who you are sending it to as part of the joke.

Building a brand on the internet can be very expensive. The founder of Moonpig, Nick Jenkins, set up the business with £150,000, raising a further £500,000 for expansion and said that it was five years before he made a profit.

◆ TIP ◆

If you intend to enter this sector then research your market carefully.

Email cards

There are a number of companies who will email a card to someone for you. As most of these are free you will need to find another way of making money to build a business. This could be by selling advertising or other products on a website.

CARD DESIGNER

Freelancers design about a third of the cards produced by the large manufacturers. So if you don't want to set up a business producing and manufacturing cards there is still a lot of scope to use your skills in this industry. You can work in any medium or style, watercolour or oil, contemporary or traditional. There is a demand for all types of work.

As a freelance artist, you can submit your works to a greeting cards design company. The advantage of being a freelance artist is that you can focus on the creation and design of the cards and let someone else worry about the production and marketing. However you still need to market yourself.

◆ TIP ◆

You don't need to write the words to go with the card as the companies usually have their own writers.

Whatever type of card you decide to produce, find out as much about the market as you can. Keep asking questions until you find the information you need. And enjoy yourself – it's great fun running a greeting cards business!

2

Handmade cards

Buying something that has been made by hand has always been a special experience. Handmade chocolates, shoes and furniture have always had a special cachet and the same can be said of handmade cards. Fortunately for makers of handmade cards there are people who are prepared to pay a little extra for something unique and very special.

WHAT TYPE OF CARD?

There are some amazing handmade cards on the market featuring a wide variety of materials and skills. From embroidery to enamelling, today's handmade cards break all the boundaries. Small makers can really challenge the big companies in this area with their flexibility and constant creativity.

There are many ways of producing handmade cards. Some require a high level of technical skill and others an eye for colour and design. All require a level of creativity and the ability to make hundreds, sometimes even thousands, of cards of the same design if you want to build a business.

HOW TO BEGIN

Starting off a handmade card business is relatively easy. Some people begin making cards when they receive a kit as a present, others have designs they want to turn into cards or want to produce something special for a friend or relative.

> ◆ TIP ◆
>
> To get an overview of the market, visit shops where you would like to sell your cards. Take note of the type of cards on sale and the prices.

FINDING INSPIRATION

A visit to a craft and hobby shop will give you some ideas of the products and materials available. There are a large number of tools available designed to help you speed up production.

If you can manage to visit one of the large craft and hobby shows (see Fact File on page 211) you should also be able to see some of the products being demonstrated; this will help you decide before committing to what can be an expensive purchase.

Whatever way you start, there is some basic equipment that is useful.

> ◆ TIP ◆
>
> Remember: time is money; you need to produce quickly and efficiently in order to build a successful business. This will involve making the best use of labour saving tools and equipment.

TOOLS

This is a list of some of the tools available on the market today. They do save time but may be expensive, so think carefully before you purchase.

Awl

This is a small pointed tool that can be used to punch small holes in paper for hand stitching.

Craft knife and metal ruler

These are essential if your cards involve cutting. Wooden rulers tend to produce shavings and soon lose their edge. Keep changing the blade on the knife to avoid dragged edges.

Eyelet-setting tool

If you are going to use eyelets in your cards you will need a special tool which rolls down the backside of the eyelet to hold it in place.

Glue brushes

Use inexpensive brushes for applying water-based liquid adhesives. Keep different sizes, use them only for glue, and rinse them out with warm water after use.

Heat gun

There are several models available and they are useful if you are going to use stamping and embossing techniques. Try and get a recommendation or see a demonstration before purchasing to make sure that you get the right model for you.

Paper trimmer or guillotine

These are essential if you want to cut pieces for layering as it is difficult to get an accurate straight cut with scissors. If you want to make your own cards they can help you save money and give you flexibility in your designs.

Ruler/square/triangle

Metal rulers are best and they keep their edges longer; a steel square is really useful for right angles and so on.

Scissors

It is worth investing in several pairs of scissors, such as a good-quality fine, precision pair for cutting paper, and ones that you don't mind getting stuck up with glue and sticky tape for everyday use. You might also find a pair of long pointed scissors, such as those used for embroidery, to be useful. If glue gets on the blade remove it before using them again. Decorative-edged scissors have a variety of uses and can provide a different look to your cards.

Scoring board and bone folder

If you are making your own cards then these are essential for a professional finish. The scoring board will help you get the proportions correct and the bone folder will give a good finish to the fold.

Sewing tools

Stitching produces beautiful results on handmade cards, and it can be done either by hand or machine. If stitching by hand you will probably need to punch holes first using a tapestry needle.

MATERIALS AND SUPPLIES

It can take some time to source the right materials and supplies, but it is important to research the market thoroughly. Many manufacturers do demonstrations at large stores and it is a good idea to attend these to increase your knowledge. When you find out which products you want to use, find a wholesale stockist or a retailer who gives discounts for quantity to help you control costs.

◆ TIP ◆

Don't skimp by buying cheap materials. Top quality cards demand top quality materials.

Adhesives

There are all sorts of different adhesives on the market and you need to try as many as possible. From double-sided tape to spray mount and adhesive sticks they all have their uses – find out which suits you. Don't forget to test its durability – you can't afford to have bits of the card dropping off.

- **PVA glue** is used for general purposes; it's permanent, holds well and dries clear.

- **Glue sticks** are good for sticking small pieces of material to a card.

- **Multi-purpose craft glue** is used for slightly heavier materials such as metal wire and charms.

- **Spray adhesive** prevents wrinkling and is good for larger pieces of material. You can also reposition it before it dries. Use in a space with good ventilation.

- **Special glues** are available for fabric and other special materials.

Card

When you are choosing the paper or card think about the weight and the surface. If, for instance, you are going to glue a lot of different objects on to the card then you will need a heavier paper. But remember that it also needs to be able to be folded properly. If you are using machine-made paper make sure that the fold goes with the grain of the paper; this is particularly important if there are several folds in the design.

Sheets of card are available in craft and art stores, stationery stores and over the internet. If you are buying over the web some suppliers sell a sample pack so you can try out a few cards before making a choice.

When developing your range you may have to make up a lot of sample cards, you will probably be able to sell these to friends and family or at a craft fair.

◆ TIP ◆

Experiment as widely as possible – time spent creating is never wasted.

Card blanks

There are many ready-made card blanks on the market produced from different weights and textures of card. Some cards have apertures cut in them so you can insert a picture behind them. Others are plain, but because they are professionally produced they give a good impression. There is a scored line down the centre and the card will therefore fold properly.

Card blanks are available in small quantities from art and craft shops and also in large quantities from wholesale suppliers. They are supplied with or without envelopes. Before you buy in quantity it is a good idea to test the types of card you intend to use; most places will provide samples or send you a sample pack for a small fee.

> **◆ KEY ◆**
>
> Cards are made from what is known as board and there are many different types (see Chapter 3). It is worth experimenting with several of these before ordering in quantity.

Cards with your logo

When you progress to supplying shops and producing in quantity you might want to have the cards printed with your business name and details on the back. Most printers will provide this service and it does add a professional finish.

Chalk inks

These are wonderful for creating backgrounds; just by swooshing across card you can create interesting effects. Again, try and get a demonstration before you purchase.

Decorative papers

The choice of papers is endless, and available in art and craft shops, stationery shops and specialist stores. Remember before buying in quantity to test them to make sure that they will stick to the surface you require, and that the colours won't run when glued. Printed with a variety of designs they can be textured, embossed or have stunning designs.

Embossing powders

To create raised surfaces you can use coloured ink with clear embossing. These fine powders come in small jars. After you sprinkle the powder onto wet pigment inks (see below), shake off the excess and return to the jar. Then use the heat gun to melt the powder and create a raised deign.

Greetings

If you are not good at lettering and don't want to hand write the greetings then you can purchase either stick-on greetings or rub-down transfers. These can have the effect of making the cards look amateurish so try and find other ways of adding a greeting if necessary. Sometimes it is possible to print the cards using a computer.

Handmade papers

Handmade papers are a good choice for distinctive cards but because of the variance in their colour and weight are not always suitable for mass-production. They can also be pricey and difficult to write on so you may have to include a sheet inside. The best use for them is probably as part of a card with a standard base.

Inkpads

These are useful for stamping designs and messages. A black one is most effective for general use.

Papers for art cards

If you are planning to paint onto the card or paper then it is important to use one which is made for this purpose. Many artists use watercolour paper, either mounting it on a traditional card or using it to make the card. Acid-free, well-sized paper with a high rag content is the best to use.

Pigment inks

You need these if you are going to emboss, as they dry more slowly than dye inks and allow you the time necessary.

Punches

There are all sorts of punches, such as round and heart shaped. They are really useful if you want to repeat a shape as well as for corner decorations. Square punches are useful for cutting windows or shapes. Other designs are useful for seasonal cards.

Recycled paper/card

There is a huge demand for products that are recycled. You can really use your imagination not only in choosing a recycled card to work on but also recycled materials, stamps, old photos, buttons and so on can all be utilised.

Rubber stamps

There are some people who make all their cards using rubber stamps but if you wish to produce a range to sell commercially you will need to use other skills to create a card which is different. Using rubber stamps may speed up the card-making process, but because they are available to everyone you run the risk of your cards looking similar to other people's. One way round this is to design your own rubber stamps.

Rubber stamps can be expensive so make sure you know what you need rather than purchasing on a whim. For decorating a series of cards, stamps are handy because you can replicate the image without much work. To slightly alter each replicated design, you can mix inks, or print only a portion of the stamp. A set of alphabet stamps is great for adding text to the card.

Sponge and cloths

Small damp sponges are good for keeping your hands clean, and you can keep your hands dry with cloths.

Stamping inks

There is a wide variety of stamping inks on the market and it is worth experimenting with different ones. Dye-based or pigment inks are best for general use. Pigment inks are thicker and used for embossing. These inks come in the form of inkpads, which you can re-ink, or bottles from which you can ink a blank pad.

Tapes

Clear double-sided tape is the easiest way to adhere decorative pieces to the cards. Foam tape is great for creating 3D effects, and pre-cut dots and squares can be an easy way to adhere small pieces of paper. 3D foam pads are useful if you want to make the card three-dimensional and there are various dispensers for sticky tapes to make life easier.

Vellum

This is a tough translucent material that comes in a variety of colours, patterns and finishes. Traditional vellum is made from animal skin and is very expensive. A more reasonably priced option is paper vellum. It can be used to veil images and create a layered effect. It is also popular to use as an enclosure in wedding invitations etc. Matching envelopes are generally available.

MASS-PRODUCING HANDMADE CARDS

To turn making handmade cards into a business you need to be able to produce them quickly and in quantity. You will only ever be able to charge so much for a handmade card – generally they retail between £3 and £6 for a standard-size card.

The speed with which you produce them is therefore critical. There are several ways in which you can speed up production:

◆ **Batch production** – apart from when you are designing cards never make only one at once. It is almost always quicker to make small quantities and carry out each process on the card for all the cards at once.

◆ **Mechanise** – where possible use die cutters, guillotines and other gadgets to speed up the process.

◆ **Simplify** – if you are producing a small number of cards and someone wants a larger order look carefully at the design and see if you can simplify. A drawn silver line instead of a stitch, for example, could save a lot of time if you are making 100 cards. Quite often the buyers won't notice the difference.

◆ **Use the quickest adhesive** and apply it properly. There are all sorts of dispensers on the market for double-sided tape, glue guns etc; investing in these can save time and your temper.

◆ **Create a proper workspace** – if you normally work on a small desk commandeer the kitchen table or other workspace for the day.

◆ **Enlist the help of friends** if you need to get an order out in a hurry. They might not be able to make the whole card but could carry out simple tasks and almost certainly label and bag the cards.

Handmade cards generally sell better in gift shops than card shops, so don't be put off if your cards fail to sell in the local shop; you might have to venture further afield to find suitable retailers.

3

Printed cards

Producing a range of printed cards is very different to producing a handmade range. Having your cards professionally printed is an exciting and scary process. It requires different skills and a substantial amount of funding. Printed cards are amongst the most popular types of cards purchased for every occasion. They are widely available and sold in a large number of different outlets, from corner shops to supermarkets to garden centres.

Producing cards for this market requires a substantial amount of capital as you need to produce them in quantity in order to make money. It is also riskier than the handmade market as if they don't sell you can be left with a lot of cards. For this reason many people start with handmade cards and learn as much as they can about the card business before targeting the printed market.

CHOOSING THE BOARD

When deciding to print cards the first thing you need to decide is what type of card to use (this is known as *board* in the industry). The choice is vast, and it is very important to choose the right board for each range of cards. Choosing by price can be a false economy as the quality of the card used will determine which market it attracts and therefore the price you can receive for it. You also need to take fashion into account and if you are using special finishes you need to know that they are going to work well on the card.

◆ KEY ◆

Discuss the various options with your printer; they know how the ink will react on the board. Listen to their advice but remember – you might have to persuade them to experiment.

If you find your printer is not very knowledgeable about board, or they have a poor selection, then you can go direct to the paper merchants (see the Fact File on page 211).

TYPES OF PRINTING

Digital printing

Initially, digital printing is good for test marketing or selling in small numbers as it is more cost effective for small quantities. However, it will be too expensive if you are intending to sell in large quantities to retailers. Also, you might notice a slight difference in the finish between litho and digital printing (see below).

Advantages of digital printing

◆ Set-up costs are cheaper because there is no need for plates as images are transferred digitally from the computer to the card. This means that you can order small quantities of high-quality full-colour prints.

◆ Useful for testing the market.

◆ Good for small runs of customised cards.

Disadvantages of digital printing

◆ Inferior print quality on large blocks of colour.

◆ Higher unit costs when producing in quantity.

◆ Digital printers cannot cope with all types of card, particularly textured and heavy weight, which may restrict your use of board.

Litho printing

Lithography is a printing process that uses chemical processes to create an image. The ink adheres to the positive image and the water cleans the negative. The print plate can be relatively flat which means that print runs can be much longer than the older methods such as engraving or embossing. As a result it is more economical when printing in quantity.

To be cost effective a print run of 2,000 is usual, which means that with a range of 30 designs you could end up with 60,000 cards to sell and store. This may sound a lot but if you are serious about marketing a printed range of cards then these are the types of quantities you are going to have to deal with.

◆ TIP ◆

Remember that unsold cards will eat into your profit margin and if not sold quickly can soon look out of date.

Advantages of litho printing

◆ Unit prices are a lot cheaper (for large print runs).

◆ This method of printing is fast and can print thousands of cards per hour.

◆ Inks are light fast.

◆ Can cope with many different finishes such as metallic and embossing.

Disadvantages of litho printing

◆ You will need a lot of capital.

SPECIAL FINISHES

There is a huge range of finishes available which can allow you to produce really unusual cards. New ones are being introduced to the market all the time so keep up to date with industry developments. Some examples are given below.

Flitter

Many modern cards are enhanced by what is known as the flitter process; during this process glitter is applied creating a more expensive finish. Alpha jewels are a special glitter cut from holographic foil.

Thermography

This is a raised finish created by heating special powder to melting point. It is very effective when combined with flitter. Vikro is another process of getting dust to fuse with ink and create texture and colour by means of thermography.

Foil embossing

This is used to create a shiny effect by stamping a hot die on to hot foil and transferring it on to the cards. This can also be done using holographic foil.

Die cutting

This is a fancy finish usually round the edges or a shape punched out with a form, which enhances the design.

The more you understand about the printing process the easier it will be to communicate effectively with your printer and therefore avoid expensive mistakes.

PRE-PRESS

Most printers have a pre-press department. This department takes the digital files and checks that they are set up correctly for manufacture. Designs are gathered together and imposed in sheet layout by positioning in a grid created in a software package. The way the cards are laid out can save you money so make sure that they are being printed the most economical way. The data is then burnt onto an aluminium plate by thermal laser ready for printing. This process is known as CTP (computer to plate). If traditional artwork is supplied it is first scanned and then the image brought together with the text and a proof supplied for approval.

◆ TIP ◆

Check proofs carefully – once you have approved them you will be responsible for payment.

PRINTING

There are many different ways of printing cards but these are the most common:

4-colour process

The images are printed using cyan, magenta, yellow and black only. In addition special colours and inks can be added to create more visual impact. These are:

fluorescent pink – this creates very bright pinks;

rhodamine red – a very bright red, popular on Christmas and Valentine cards;

metallic – metallic colours are now very popular and there is a huge range available;

coatings and varnishes – special finishes can be applied depending on the board that has been used. These can be applied over the whole board or selectively.

◆ TIP ◆

Remember that as the front and back are printed together it will be possible to have colour on the back without occurring any extra costs. This can add value to the product.

Hexachrome

This is a printing technique that uses a special six-colour set of inks, which provide a very broad colour spectrum. Hexachrome is typically used where clean oranges, pinks, purples and greens are required to reproduce artwork subjects. They are not recommended for photographic reproductions.

MetalFX

This is a relatively new technology launched in 2002. The MetalFX processes over a 104 million metalised shades of colour using the process set and one metallic colour. The software enables special effects and holographic style images which were previously very expensive to be created within the design process. Not all printers are licensed to use this process.

Digital print

The technology takes the digital artwork and converts it into a printed image on the correct scheme without the need to make printing plates. As a result it is very economical for small runs. It can be combined with other software to produce personalised versions of the cards. It is used extensively by the trade for sample runs to enable them to assess the sales potential of new card ranges economically. The digital print can be finished in the same way as the litho print to create an exact version.

FINISHING

Cards can be finished in a variety of ways.

Four-page card

This is a card folded once; the back page can be slightly undercut so it doesn't show when folded.

Six-page card

A card folded twice. It is often used with die cutting to hold artwork or photographs in place.

French fold or eight-page card

A card folded twice in two different directions.

Tipped-in insert

A paper insert is glued into the spine of a card, or can alternatively be glued to page three. This process can be carried out by hand or machine. The insert must be at least 4 mm smaller than the card to allow for a border.

Gate-fold card

A six-page card where four of the six pages meet at the front of the card, generally at the centre of the card's finished width, although the 'gate' folds can also be left short to reveal the design inside.

Concertina or 'Z'-fold card

A card that is folded at least twice, then back on itself in a concertina fashion.

Short-fold card

A card where one of the pages is shorter than the overall finished size of the card.

Landscape card

When viewed this stands on its longest side.

Portrait card

This stands on its shortest side.

Tent-fold card

This has the fold at the top.

Face side

This is normally the name given to the printed side of the card, but can also refer to the coated side.

Reverse side

The opposite of the above, also the uncoated side.

Die cutting

Die cutting is a process for cutting cards to size. It uses the pressure of a die cutting press and a cutting form made to fit the precise requirements of the printed sheet or individual card. It cuts one sheet at a time and therefore is more precise than guillotining.

Die cutting can also be used to describe the cutting out of shapes within a card.

Deckled edges

A wavy or ragged edge to a card. There are many standard patterns available or you can have your own made, although this can be expensive.

Apertures

These are holes within the body of the card that require cutting out. They are limited by the strength of the board remaining.

EMBOSSING

The process for indenting the surface of a board/paper by use of pressure, this is used to form a raised image using a male and female die. This process can be done on an individual card basis or the same size as a printed sheet.

Graining/grain emboss

This puts an overall pattern onto a sheet on plain board and is an excellent way of creating texture.

Flitter, glitter, virko and thermo

Flitter is adhered to selected areas of the card to create a decorative and reflective image. The generic name for these processes is thermography.

Foils and foiling

There are many different types of foil, geared to various applications. Typically, greeting cards' publishers use metallic, pigmented (i.e. non-metallic coloured) foils, opaque, translucent, pearliest and holographic foils.

Fixtures, fittings and attachments

These terms are used to describe things that are attached to the card, usually by hand. This could be anything from a fridge magnet or badge to woven patches or anything mounted on to the card, such as jewellery. This is usually a manual process and can therefore add considerably to the cost of the product.

FINDING A PRINTER

Finding a printer can be one of the most important things you do in setting up the business. You need to be very involved with the printer at every stage which means that it is important you choose carefully.

Printers are not necessarily the most creative people nor do they always communicate well, so it's up to you to ask the right questions and to let the printer have all the information they need. Finding a good printer is not always easy. Personal recommendation is useful but try and find one who is interested in your type of business. Printers are notorious for late delivery so allow plenty of time between you receiving the cards and the orders needing to be sent out.

You should obtain quotes from several printers, go and visit and talk to them and always choose one who you are comfortable working with. Ask lots of questions and learn basic techniques – you need to know what can be done in order to do it. Most printers are happy to explain their craft providing you go at a quiet time.

 KEY ◆

There is a list of technical terms used by printers at the back of the book.

To place an order

◆ Always write down exactly what you want.

◆ Check that the quote matches what you asked for; ask about extras such as delivery charges.

◆ Find out the size of sheet the printers are planning to use and see if you can use it more effectively.

You will need to decide:

◆ The size of the cards: will they be portrait or landscape.

◆ How many cards you will need to print.

◆ What type and weight of paper you will use.

◆ How copy will be provided: original artwork or disc?

◆ Style of text.

◆ Do you require your cards to be creased and folded? Creasing is vital but you may want to do the folding yourself to save money.

◆ Are your cards to be varnished?

◆ KEY ◆

Confirm dates for proofing and delivery, write them down and check with the printer a couple of days before each to ensure you haven't been forgotten. This is particularly important if you have supply deadlines.

◆ TIP ◆

When you find a good printer work with them and treat them well. They can make the difference between success and failure for your business.

Proofs

It is vital that you check the proofs yourself. Always insist on a wet proof as this will give a good indication of the finished version. A wet proof gives the actual colours which will appear rather than an indication of the colour. Check carefully for marks and compare the original against the proof, although you might prefer the proof.

Producing a printed range of cards can be a really exciting experience. Mistakes will be made but learn from them, and keep going.

Prices

Traditionally, printed cards were always at the cheaper end of the market but with improved finishes and exciting innovations this is no longer true and printed cards can command a higher price than they used to.

Once you become familiar with the printing process and have confidence in your printer, the speed with which you can produce cards can be very fast. Don't forget that you will need to have somewhere to store them!

4

Designing cards

HOW TO BECOME A CARD DESIGNER

If you are good at designing cards but don't want the hassle of running a business then you can try and sell your designs. As a freelance artist you submit your work to a greeting cards company and they produce and market them to retailers.

The advantage of this is that you can focus on the creation and design of the cards. The disadvantage is that the company has control over the finished aspect of the cards. Some artists find it difficult to have their work used in this way. Others find it combines the best of both worlds – their cards are published and they spend time doing what they really want to do – creating the artwork.

◆ KEY ◆

> The market for card designs is huge but to be successful you need to target your market carefully, making sure that you submit the right designs to the right company.

What type of work do they want?

While some publishers concentrate on producing a certain type of greeting card, e.g. fine art, the majority publish a variety of ranges. It is therefore important that you research the market properly to avoid wasting your time and theirs.

The work required falls broadly into the following categories:

◆ artwork

◆ humorous ideas

◆ verses.

Artwork is required for a wide variety of cards such as cute, contemporary, fine art, photographic, traditional and children's. A look around any specialist greeting cards shop will illustrate the wide variety of artwork used.

◆ TIP ◆

Don't use well-known characters; they will certainly by protected by copyright.

Humorous ideas can be anything from jokes to cartoons and punch lines. The artwork doesn't have to be great as it is the idea the publisher will be looking at, so anything that would make a great card is worth submitting. Apparently, finding people with ideas that will make others laugh is very difficult, so if you can do this you should have a great opportunity.

Verses are not used by all card companies so make sure you target the right ones. Those that do produce cards with words need a never-ending supply of verses so if you are skilled in writing copy or poems this could be a great market for you. There are generally three styles of writing in greeting cards: verse, prose and punch lines.

Whatever your skill there is probably a market that is right for you. One card company, Simon Elvin, produces 2,000 different designs each year using artwork, humour and verses. They constantly need new talent; the market for new ideas is huge – why not give it a go?

FINDING A GREETING CARDS COMPANY

To find greeting cards companies check out the website of the Greeting Card Association (www.greetingcardassociation.org.uk) or visit a card shop and find a range of cards you like. Take note of the publishers and look them up on the internet – their websites often have details of how to send in designs. Alternatively, publications such as *Greetings Today* and *Progressive Greetings* often advertise for card designers and also carry advertisements for artists looking for work.

You can choose to submit your work to the major companies or you can start with smaller companies. This will allow you to learn the ropes in terms of working with editors, tackling assignments and meeting deadlines. But be warned, competition is fierce and you will need to persevere if you are to survive. Some artists also find that they are asked to change their colours and designs to fit in with the company's ranges and if you are not comfortable with this then steer clear of this market.

◆ TIP ◆

If you are worried about your designs being copied then read the chapter on copyright at the end of the book.

There are over 400 card companies exhibiting at the Spring Fair in Birmingham every year so there are plenty to try. Small companies or one-man bands will generally not be worth approaching as they do all their own designing, but keep watch for those that are growing.

HOW TO SUBMIT WORK

Step 1: Research the market

Firstly, you need to identify the companies that manufacture cards which suit your style. It is no use wasting your or their time by submitting humour cards to a fine art company, or vice versa.

To identify the right companies browse the greeting cards in a variety of stores from WH Smith to the independent gift shops. This will give you a good picture of the type of cards on sale. You can either note down the names of the publishers or purchase a number of cards where the artists work in a similar style. You will then have the details of the companies and time to examine the cards in detail.

Good publishers' websites to look at are

www.artgroup.com

www.abacuscards.co.uk

www.paperhouse.co.uk

www.simonelvin.co.uk

Step 2: Prepare some designs, ideas or verses

If you are chosen to design cards the company will give you a brief, so you do not need to submit a whole range to a company. They are more interested in the ideas and your ability to work with them. If you are not a brilliant artist but have a lot of creative ideas don't be afraid of submitting them as they will have in-house artists who will work on them and they may just buy the idea.

When designing think about the size and shape of the card. Square and unusually shaped cards can cause problems in the export market as postal regulations overseas vary. Check that your cards conform to UK postal regulations and that they will fit into a stand or spinner so that they can be displayed properly. Also remember that the bit of the card the customer sees first in a card rack is the top!

Step 3: Submitting your work

Contact the companies that interest you and ask them if they have guidelines for submitting work (sometimes these are published on the website). If writing always enclose a stamped addressed envelope, or contact them by email. Once you have the guidelines follow them exactly

– if they say they only require comic cards then don't bother sending them floral designs. They know what they want.

Step 4: The submission

Send several examples of your work to show the breadth of your artistic skills. Some publishers prefer to see finished designs, others well-presented sketches. A publisher is usually looking for a distinctive style, creative thinking, knowledge of the market and a professional approach. It is a good idea to include at least one design in colour to aid visualisation.

Step 5: Feedback

Some publishers respond straight away, others on a monthly basis. Don't harass them, and don't get disheartened. They may contact you and ask for more submissions which are more specific, but they will not expect to pay you at this stage, as it is speculative.

Trade fairs

Some publishers are willing to meet artists at trade fairs, others are not (see Fact File for a list of trade fairs at the end of the book). If you want to approach a particular company then make sure they are exhibiting at that fair. Visit the fair at the end of the week when it's quieter and approach them on the stand. Have a few samples available, and if you believe your work is relevant for them ask them for a contact number or name. Have some cards available with your details and an image and leave these with them. Trade fairs are hectic events and things do get lost so it's a good idea to still submit your work by post or email.

What format?

Never send original work at this stage, send good quality prints. They will usually ask for 6 to 12 images. Never send work you need returned; as it may get lost in a busy office. Good quality colour photocopies, photo-graphs or computer printouts are generally acceptable as are digital files (Jpegs are fine) on CD Rom. Ideas for humorous cards or verses can be sent in the same way. Make sure everything is clearly labelled with your name and contact details.

How many?

Companies receive a lot of submissions and they are very good at spotting the artists who will fit into their design team. Be guided by the information you receive from each company but as a general rule send 12 images.

> ◆ TIP ◆
>
> It is important to target more than one company at once. It is not easy to take rejection so having more than one application on the go will help you keep positive. Don't forget to send different samples to each company, and while you are waiting keep designing.

Top tips for submitting work

Dos

◆ Do your research. Time spent examining the market will save you time and money in the long run.

◆ Always check if a company accepts work from freelancers and check what format they require.

◆ Remember that the top half of the design is the most important.

◆ Leave room for a caption if you are targeting this type of range.

◆ Put your contact details on everything you send in, in case it gets separated.

- Always meet deadlines.

- Present everything properly.

- Do enclose a large SAE with enough postage if you want your work returned, but realise that in a busy office it may get lost, so keep copies of everything.

- Do be prepared to discuss payment.

Don'ts

- Don't ever send originals.

- Don't be long-winded; long letters rarely get read.

- Don't sell the same designs to two publishers.

- Don't take rejection personally. Ask for feedback; some companies give it others don't.

What is a range?

Before any artist engaged by a company puts pen to paper the company will issue them with guidelines as to how many cards there will be within the range and how many they expect them to design. Usually one artist is assigned to each range but a group of artists could work on a themed range.

Design brief

A design brief is drawn up and issued to the artist who then come up with some ideas. If these are suitable they will be expanded to more detailed designs before the artist embarks on the final piece of artwork.

How long should it take?

All artists work at different speeds but it is unlikely that a design should take more than two days although this may be spread over a period of time if the designs are sent back for alteration.

How much do they pay?

A fee is negotiated for the worldwide reproduction rights of each design separately. This usually lasts from the date of publication until the design is discontinued. Exact figures are difficult to come by as freelance artists are dealt with individually. Obviously, well-known artists can command higher fees.

Payments and contracts depend on individual companies but it is not unusual for the designer of a card which sells in the millions at Christmas to receive a design fee of between £200 and £250. Unless you are a well-known artist like David Hockney, when you can sell your designs under licence, you will only receive a design fee.

THE MARKET

There are cards for every conceivable occasion and new ones are being brought out all the time. The following lists will give you some idea of the ranges available.

◆ TIP ◆

85 to 90 per cent of cards are purchased by women.

Birthday cards

The most popular cards bought are birthday cards; they cover all ages and types of people:

- ◆ ages 1–12 for children

- ◆ age 13 – now you are a teenager

- ◆ age 18

- ◆ age 21

- ◆ ages 30, 40, 50, 60, 65, 70, 80, 90, 95 and 100.

◆ TIP ◆
50 per cent of the market is for birthday cards.

General cards

Featuring all types of subject from flowers to sport to landscape, there are cards available for almost every interest and mood. Many of these are left blank so they can be used for birthdays, occasions or simply to send a message.

Blank cards

Increasing in popularity, particularly amongst younger people, blank cards allow people to write their own message. Photographic cards and art cards that can be framed are amongst the most popular blank cards.

Occasions

There is a vast range of occasion cards including the following:

anniversary	bon voyage	christening
Christmas	congratulations	driving test
Easter	examination	Father's Day

get well	good luck	leaving
love & friendship	Mother's Day	new baby
new home	new job	new school
retirement	sorry	sympathy
thank you	Thanksgiving	thinking of you
Valentine's Day	wedding	

Within these categories there are numerous variations; don't just think of birthday cards but remember all the other opportunities. Don't forget niche markets such as Yom Kippur, St Patrick's Day, and Eid.

♦ TIP ♦

Remember that publishers work a long time in advance. Christmas is launched in January to retailers and the other seasons at least six months in advance.

THE MONEY

There are no definite rules for payment. Artists are paid in several different ways and can be paid on design or range basis. The most common methods of payment are:

Flat fee

The publisher makes a one-off payment to the artist for ownership of a design for an unlimited period. This fee will normally be between £150–£250 for one single design. The unit fee usually reduces if a range is to be produced.

Licensing fee

This allows the publisher the right to use artwork for specified types of products and for a specific number of years, after which the rights revert to the artist. Artists are paid in the region of £150 + per design for this.

Licensing fee + royalty

This is similar to the above, but with a royalty payment on each card sold. Artists generally receive £100 + licensing fee plus 3 per cent of the trade price of each card sold.

Advance royalty deal

The artist is paid a goodwill advance on royalties. In the case of a range, the artist would receive a goodwill advance of, say, £500–£1,000, and then receive an additional royalty payment of 5 per cent once the threshold is reached.

Royalty only

The artist receives regular royalty payments based on the number of cards sold. Royalties are generally paid quarterly. Artists should expect a sales report and a royalty statement.

Making your portfolio

If companies are interested in your work they may ask you to visit them with a portfolio. Again, target this at the company. Feature work that is likely to fit into their range, present it professionally and have some material to leave with them. Try and find out what format they prefer: original work, CD and so on.

Contents for a general portfolio

◆ 20 high quality images of your most current work. This can be original work or good quality prints. You can also include a CD with this work on it.

◆ Copies of published work (if applicable).

◆ CV or personal statement.

Remember:

◆ All work should be current.

◆ Slides should be viewed easily.

◆ Put your best work first and show a consistent style.

◆ Presentation is almost as important as content; make sure all your work is clean, tidy and labelled.

◆ KEY ◆

Adjust your portfolio for each company. Try and find out what they want to see and make your portfolio fit their brief.

5

Art and photographic cards

Many artists and photographers decide to sell their work as greeting cards to increase their income and also to build their reputation. Some have their work chosen by the larger card companies and this can lead to national exposure. Glasgow artist Jack Vettriano's work has definitely increased in value since his cards were produced for the mass market and the general public became aware of his work.

Even selling your cards in a small way can help increase your profile and make people more aware of your work.

There are two ways of having your work produced as cards:

◆ selling your photographs, or art work to a major company

◆ producing and selling your own cards.

SELLING TO A LARGE PUBLISHER

The first route has been covered in the chapter on designing cards; simply follow the same procedure in contacting card companies with samples of your work. You will not have as much control over your work but you will reach a wider market.

Remember to find out if companies are interested in original artwork or photographic cards, if they're not then no matter how good your work is you are wasting your time. Also try and come up with something new rather than rehashing an already existing range.

PRODUCING ORIGINAL CARDS

This chapter is about how to produce and sell your own work as greeting cards. One mistake that artists and photographers sometimes make is that they assume that the work they sell as large images will automatically reproduce well as a card. Some do and some don't and you need to be quite ruthless in deciding what to use. (Don't be put off if you don't think your current work will sell well as cards. It might be quite an exciting challenge to produce work that fits a different format.)

Ideas to try

1. Many artists have made a significant contribution to their income by **cutting up 'failed' paintings** and making them into cards. Every painting will have some part of it that works and this can often be made into a great card. Although it can be quite time-consuming, they are original works of art and the prices can reflect this. Many people actually buy this type of card and frame it, so if you are exhibiting at a fair you can sell frames alongside to generate extra income.

2. Having **artwork made into prints** is also a good way of producing a saleable product. With the sophisticated printing equipment and computers available for home use you can do this yourself. Alternatively, for small print runs, you can use a digital printer.

3. Another cost-effective method is to **put several images on one A4 sheet** and have it colour photocopied onto glossy paper. This produces a good image at a reasonable cost and is a service available at many high street printers and large office suppliers.

4. Colour photographic images are easy to produce. Why not try something different: **black and white photographs** can be very popular. If you have access to a darkroom they are cheap to produce; if you don't have the facilities try joining a class – you can usually use the facilities at quiet times.

5. **Producing a range of local views** may not be the most inspiring work artistically, but can be very lucrative – particularly in tourist areas. If producing local cards for the tourist market in your area works you might be able to repeat it elsewhere.

6. If you are producing original artwork don't paint it straight onto the card. Use paper and then **spray mount the image** onto the card, this reduces cost and wastage.

7. A limited type of mass production can work, some artists **paint simple watercolours 10 at a time** to save time. This can be boring but lucrative.

8. Make sure the **people who buy the cards can contact you**. These types of cards tend to be kept, and when the customer can afford an original piece of work you want them to know where they can find you.

9. **A good range of cards** can enhance your profile and help you build a reputation.

Digitally enhanced photographs

There is much debate as to whether you should label your work if it is digitally enhanced. Sometimes this is obvious, other times not so. This is really personal preference although you may find that if you are selling through galleries they insist that the work is accurately labelled.

PRINTING YOUR OWN CARDS

There are various ways of printing your own cards using home computer equipment such as a laser or inkjet printer. There is a wide variety of papers available which give unusual surfaces and this can give your work an interesting perspective and stop it looking homemade.

If you want to produce an even more professional print of a higher quality, you could consider using a process known as giclée printing. Setting up can be expensive, but often a group of artists will get together and purchase the equipment. As the equipment is made to run constantly this is an effective way to operate.

Giclée printing

The advantages of using giclée are that the colour range is wider and the purity of colour much better. Once again there are a number of different papers to use and you have direct control over the process so you may feel that you are creating a work of art. On the other hand, apart from the cost of the equipment, you do need to learn how to operate the machinery which is not that easy, and you may think that your time could be better spent actually producing original work. In that case the key is to find a giclée printer who understands your work and how you want it reproduced.

COMMERCIALLY PRODUCED PHOTOGRAPHS

Although it is possible to have your photographs produced on a printer at home you might find it more cost-effective to use a commercial printer. In addition to the high street chains there are several websites which offer this service.

OUTLETS FOR YOUR WORK

Art and photographic cards are not generally sold in normal card shops so you need to be creative when looking for outlets. In addition to selling beside your work at art fairs try some of the following:

Galleries

Some galleries do not sell cards at all. Others have a far more flexible attitude, particularly if the artist is already exhibiting at the gallery. They rarely have card stands so be prepared to offer some form of display stand in order to get them to try your cards.

Garden centres

Garden centres usually have cards related to their product so if you paint flowers or have fantastic photographs of gardens on your cards this could be an excellent outlet for you. Be aware that garden centres are not always the cleanest of places – make sure your cards are well wrapped and if they are on sale or return be prepared to change the cello wrap if they are returned.

Tourist Information Centres

TICs are always on the lookout for local products. If you photograph local beauty spots or paint local watercolours that can be made into prints you should find a ready market. They may ask for postcards, but be careful – the financial return on postcards is very small and you will have to sell a substantial number to make it worthwhile.

Theatre foyers

There has been a move in recent years for theatre and concert halls to have shops to help them increase their income. If your work is related to this environment then you should be able to command premium prices from well-heeled customers.

Specialist shops

Again, depending on your subject matter you may find a ready market at specialist shops such as florists or chocolate shops. You might have to provide your own stand but it can be a good market.

Tourist attractions

Wildlife sanctuaries, zoos and other tourist attractions can be a good market if your work reflects the image of the attraction.

PRICING

The average market rate for this type of card is between £2.95 and £5. This may seem like a good return but remember that if you are selling via shops and galleries you will only receive between £1.50 and £2.50. This may seem like a lot of commission but they are doing the selling for you, and if they are turning over a large number of cards it can still be lucrative.

In the right setting artwork or photographic cards can fetch up to £10, particularly if people believe they are buying a work of art. Research your market carefully – don't waste your time producing cheap cards if there is a better market out there.

◆ TIP ◆

Don't forget that selling the cards yourself at fairs is by far the most financially rewarding.

Purchasing materials in bulk can save a lot of money: card, envelope and cello wrap can cost as little as 20p per card for good quality.

Calculating prices

It is difficult to cost out the time making the artwork or taking the photographs but it is possible to work out how long it will take you to make a batch of cards. Try and make a minimum of 50 cards at one go, stamping, labelling, glueing and signing. Time how long it takes you, decide how you much you want to earn an hour, and add this to the material costs of the cards.

For example

Materials	20p
Time taken for 50 cards	3 hours @ £6 an hour = 36p per card
Cost of card	56p

If you can sell this to a gallery for £1.50 this will give you a reasonable return. If you are selling via craft and art fairs you will incur extra costs but you will also be able to charge more.

TOP TIPS FOR ART AND PHOTOGRAPHIC CARDS

1. A signature adds value to the product.

2. Good labelling tells the customer exactly what they are getting.

3. Stamping the envelope or the back of the card adds authenticity.

4. Enclosing an order form can lead to repeat sales.

5. Purchase materials in bulk to keep costs down.

6. Batch produce the cards to control time.

7. Ask galleries for advice on pricing.

8. Initially target a specific sector such as landscape, floral or abstract.

9. Test the market by going to a craft/art fair.

10. Produce a show card for galleries.

◆ KEY ◆

Try and produce something different. Originality will be your unique selling point, but always bear in mind that if someone likes your card it could become the company Christmas card and they may want to order 100!

6

Starting a business

When starting a business it's easy to get carried away with the creative side of designing, making and selling the cards and forget that in order for it to run you must do certain things to ensure that your business is legal and organised properly.

Setting everything up from the start will make it easier as your business grows, so spend some time thinking and planning the best way for you to operate.

TYPES OF BUSINESS

Firstly you need to decide how you are going to trade. Basically, there are five types of business structures.

- sole trader

- partnership

- limited company

- co-operative

- social enterprise.

Sole trader

Sole trader is the term used for a one-person business with or without employees. It is the easiest, and therefore the most common, form of business start-up.

For tax and National Insurance purposes you are self-employed – i.e. any profits, including wages drawn, are taxed at personal rates.

Advantages of being a sole trader

◆ you only need to register as self-employed

◆ inexpensive to set up

◆ no need for accounts to be audited

◆ lower NI contributions.

Disadvantages

◆ you are personally liable for all your business debts

◆ some NI benefits are not available

◆ can be difficult to get credit.

Partnership

A partnership is similar to that of a sole trader except that two or more people own the business. All partners are jointly liable for debts so it is vital that you choose your partner with care.

It is also important that you have a partnership agreement, which should be drawn up by a solicitor. To save money, identify what you want in a partnership agreement before going to a solicitor as this will save time. You should also consider how you are going to end the partnership if it doesn't work as this can cause real problems.

Partnership agreement

A partnership agreement should contain:

1. name and address of the partners

2. start date and firm's name

3. business activities and location

4. premises agreement – if applicable

5. capital – details on how the business is going to be financed

6. the profits (loss) of the business: how is this going to be split

7. what drawings the partners are going to take

8. restrictive covenants – if there are any restrictions on the activities of the partners e.g. working for someone else

9. accountant and banking details

10. role of the partners

11. how disputes are going to be solved

12. pension arrangements

13. admission of new partners

14. who will do what

15. partnership meetings and voting rights

16. details about ending the partnership.

It is often the last clause that causes the most problems. Ending a business partnership is like ending a marriage – never easy. The clearer this section is the easier it will be for one partner to carry on the business should the other decide to leave.

Advantages of a partnership

◆ it can spread the risks

◆ it can offer support, especially during difficult times

◆ there may be more finance available

◆ two people can bring in extra skills.

Disadvantages

◆ you could be responsible for your partner's debts

◆ need to draw up an agreement – can be expensive

◆ could fall out with partner and lose a friend as well as a business partner.

Limited company

It is possible to set up a limited company yourself by applying for a starter pack from Companies House. It is, however, simpler to pass the job on to a solicitor, accountant or a specialist company.

In a limited company the personal liability of the owners for the debt of the company is limited to the nominal value of the shareholding (your personal assets are not included).

To set up a limited company you also need a company secretary. Be careful who you choose – even if they only have a nominal role it can be difficult if you fall out. Until recently there were substantial tax benefits in being a limited company, but this is no longer the case. It is a good idea to discuss this with your accountant as setting up a limited company may not be in your best interests at this stage.

◆ A limited company is a separate legal entity and therefore can sue and be sued.

◆ You are not self-employed but employed as a director by the company.

◆ As a director you pay tax under PAYE and have NI deducted from your earnings.

◆ The company pays corporation tax on its profits.

Co-operative

A co-operative is owned and controlled by the people working in it, each of whom can be a member having an equal share and an equal voting right. Some people like the ethics behind forming a co-operative, others find it difficult to work in a situation where in effect major decisions are taken by a committee.

There are four ways of forming a co-operative

1. You can form a partnership. The disadvantage of this is that there is no limited liability; the business could also be sold for the benefit of its members which is against the fundamental principle of a co-operative.

2. You can form a limited company, but again the aims of a limited company are not always the same as those of a co-operative.

3. The most usual way of forming a co-operative is to seek registration with the Financial Services Authority as a co-operative. The

Co-operative Union can help with setting up a new co-operative and can speed up the process.

4. You can organise the co-operative as a company limited by guarantee. This needs only two people to form it.

Advantages of being a co-operative

◆ encourages participation in the business and shared responsibility

◆ workforce more motivated

◆ shared decision-making

◆ network of support available

◆ profits shared amongst the workforce i.e. not shareholders.

Disadvantages of being a co-operative

◆ can be difficult to find the right people

◆ decision-making can take longer

◆ rewards are spread out amongst the members.

Social Enterprise

In the last couple of years a new type of business has come to prominence in the UK, known as Social Enterprises. They are businesses with primarily social objectives whose surpluses are principally reinvested for that purpose in the business or the community rather than being driven by the need to make profits for owners or shareholders.

Social Enterprises tackle a wide range of social and environmental issues and operate in all parts of the economy. They work by using business solutions to revitalise communities and help people find work. They aim to revitalise and help create sustainable communities using traditional methods of commercial businesses.

Why Social Enterprise?

One of the reasons this sector is receiving so much publicity is that it seems to combine the glamour of the commercial sector with the caring for the community that most people consider important. One result of the government being very supportive of Social Enterprises is that they have put considerable resources into the sector, which means that it should be easier to find funding to set up a business in this way than many others.

Basically, Social Enterprises have three common characteristics:

1. **Focus** – they are directly involved in producing goods or providing services to a market. They actively seek to be viable trading operations and to make a profit.

2. **Social aims** – they also have specific social aims such as job creation, training or providing local services. They are committed to supporting their local community and have strong ethical values.

3. **They are autonomous organisations** governed by stakeholder groups or trustees with profits being distributed back into the organisation, amongst the 'shareholders', or used for the benefit of the community.

Some examples of Social Enterprise are craft marketing co-operatives, studio groups, guilds and artist associations.

Further helpful information can be found at www.unltd.org.uk and www.socialenterprisemag.co.uk. Running a Social Enterprise is not an easy option – you have to make money and fulfil a social need – but it can be an exciting and fulfilling way to do business.

How to decide which type of business

A **limited company** has several advantages: limited liability, greater credibility, lower tax, better pension rules, more avenues for raising finance and easier disposal of part of your business. However it costs more to set up than being a sole trader or partnership, and you really need an accountant to handle your accounts.

A **sole trader** and **partnership** have much simpler administration arrangements, fewer difficult rules about accounts, and better tax treatment of losses.

If you are forming any type of **partnership** you really do need a partnership agreement drawn up by a solicitor.

The simplest way to start is as a **sole trader**; you can always convert to one of the others as you grow.

If you want your business to help the community then consider setting up a **Social Enterprise**.

Examples of different types of businesses

Sole trader

Setting up a handmade greeting cards business from the kitchen table.

Partnership

Two or more people who want to go into business together but keep it simple.

Limited company

You plan to rent premises and inject a large amount of capital having a range of cards printed to supply leading retailers.

Co-operative

A group of artists who get together and form a co-operative to market their cards.

Social Enterprise

Setting up a business enabling people with disabilities to produce and retail cards.

YOU AND THE TAXMAN

When you first start in business you must register with HM Revenue and Customs (HMRC). You can do this in a number of different ways:

◆ call the help line for self-employed on 08459 154515

◆ complete the CWF1 form online at www.workingforyourself.co.uk/selfemployed/form.asp.

 TIP ◆

Remember: you must register within three months of the end of the month in which you start up.

If you do not register within this time you may be liable to a penalty of £100. It is a mistake to try and get away with not registering – it is becoming increasingly easy to find people who are trading and not registering. If you are in any doubt, the tax office has a help line and they are more user friendly than they used to be.

National Insurance Contribution (NIC)

As a self-employed person you pay a fixed amount of class 2 National Insurance (NIC). If your profits are above a certain limit you may also pay Class 4.

Currently the Class 2 is £2.30 per week.

If your net profit is low you can apply for an exemption but this could affect your state benefits e.g. pension.

Keeping records

Whatever type of business you set up it is very important that all records, receipts and so on are retained. You need to keep them for seven years. Set up a system as soon as possible to:

◆ record and keep copies of all sales and other business receipts

◆ separately record any money from the sale of any business assets

◆ record all purchases of business stock as you buy it

◆ keep a record of all business expenses, no matter how small. They soon add up and may be tax deductible

◆ keep all bank records including cheque stubs and paying in books

◆ keep records of all 'wages' and amounts drawn out of the business for personal use

◆ record all money that you put into the business

◆ keep all business bills, invoices and paperwork (stick small receipts onto large pieces of paper for safe-keeping)

◆ keep a record of the miles you do for the business

◆ keep a list of all capital items bought and sold.

Under self-assessment you are required to send the Inland Revenue a tax return each year and to pay your tax bill by the due date. You will be sent a self-assessment form in April.

VAT

You don't have to register for VAT until your annual taxable turnover reaches £60,000 (September 2007). For more information visit the Customs and Excise website www.hmce.gov.uk or call the National Advice Service 0845 010 9000.

INSURANCE

Whatever type of business you start you will need insurance. Depending on what you are doing there are different types of business insurance.

Types of insurance

◆ Insurance to cover risks and disaster.

◆ Employers' liability – if you have employees.

◆ Motor insurance – if you have a vehicle.

◆ Public/product liability – if you have premises or intend to exhibit at fairs then you will almost certainly need this type of insurance.

◆ Legal expenses.

◆ Copyright protection.

If you belong to a professional association such as the CGA, the Giftware Association, or your local Chamber of Trade, you may be covered for certain types of insurance so check before you take out more.

Loss of earnings insurance

You can insure against loss of earnings, but it is expensive. It may be worth doing if you have a family depending on you for their income. A more sensible option is to calculate how much money you need to pay the bills for three months. Before you start up in business save this amount and put it in a separate account – it will provide you with security.

PENSIONS

There are special rules that cover the self-employed and directors of companies. When you are setting up a business the last thing you are thinking of is your pension, but as soon as money becomes available you should start to make pension provision in one way or another. To set up a pension plan it is a good idea to seek advice from your accountant or financial advisor.

HEALTH AND SAFETY

It is your responsibility to provide a reasonable standard of health and safety for your employees, for visitors and members of the public who may be affected, and also for you.

An inspector has the right to enter your workplace to examine it and enforce legal requirements even if that place is also your home.

EMPLOYMENT LAW

As your business grows you may need to employ people, in which case you need to be up to date with current employment legislation including minimum wage, holiday and sick leave etc. You will also be required to carry employment liability insurance. Contact www.dti.gov.uk/employment.

Other relevant legislation

You will also need to be aware of the following laws that affect all UK businesses.

◆ **The Sale of Goods Act** 1979 (as amended by the Sale and Supply of Goods Act 1994), which stipulates that products supplied to consumers must be of satisfactory quality, and entitles the consumer to a refund if this is not the case.

◆ **General Product Safety Regulations** 2005, which outline minimum safety standards for products supplied to consumers.

◆ **Consumer Protection Act** 1987, which regulates liability for damage, including death or personal injury, caused by defective products.

◆ **Trade Descriptions Act** 1968, which prevents you from advertising a product or service you cannot actually supply.

For information on all the above legislation contact your local Trading Standards office or visit their website at www.tradingstandards.gov.uk.

7

Writing a business plan

A business plan is a road map for your business. It tells you where you want to go and how you intend to get there.

WHY WRITE A BUSINESS PLAN?

There are two main reasons for writing a business plan. Firstly, to explain to outsiders such as banks what you are planning to do, and to help you raise money from grants and loans. Secondly, to use within the business to help you remember what you want to achieve, and to remind you at busy times the direction you really want to go in. It is about the facts and figures involved in your business but it is also about your vision, your ideas and your enthusiasm.

Starting a small business can be very time-consuming: producing the product, finding the outlets, locating suppliers. Spending some time planning how you are going to do everything will save time in the long term.

Who will want to see my plan?

If you are borrowing money to set up your business then the bank or finance organisation will almost certainly want to see a business plan. They may also want it in a certain format so check this out before you write your plan. The high street banks all supply CDs and information on how to write business plans. If you are applying for studio space or a place in an incubator unit they may also want to see a copy of your plan.

So whether you need a business plan to raise finance, rent premises, or whether it is just for your own use, make writing it a priority.

◆ TIP ◆

Time spent planning is never wasted.

Why do you need to plan?

Starting your own business is an exciting, challenging activity and the last thing you want to do when you are being carried away by the dream is to think about planning. However, just as you wouldn't set out on a journey without some idea of the direction in which you are going, you shouldn't embark on setting up a business without a plan.

◆ KEY ◆

If you fail to plan you plan to fail.

The reason many people give for not planning is that it is too restrictive. They want to be free to change their minds and go in different directions. But a business plan is not set in stone – it is a working tool that should be reviewed and updated regularly. One of the challenges of running your own business is that it is constantly changing and the business plan needs to reflect this.

GETTING HELP WITH WRITING YOUR PLAN

If you are unsure how to start and think you would benefit from some help there are several sources available. Some of these may be free, others you will have to pay for.

Businesslink

A telephone call to your local Businesslink should tell you if there is any help available in your area (www.businesslink.gov.uk).

Local Enterprise Agency

Most areas have an Enterprise Agency. You can find them through Businesslink or the Federation of Enterprise Agencies website www.nfea.com. Sometimes local councils fund organisations which help businesses to start up. Councils usually have a local economic unit which offers help and support to commercial businesses. A phone call to the local council offices should help you identify who to contact.

LearnDirect

LearnDirect offers computer based courses on how to write a business plan, these can be useful for people who are setting up while still working as it allows you to do them in your own time. There is information on www.learndirect.co.uk.

Bank

Your bank will certainly have a business plan available in either CD format or hard copy. If you are looking to open a business account ask all the banks you are considering what help they offer.

Accountant/financial advisor

An accountant or financial advisor will help you put together the figures and some offer a complete business plan service, but this can be expensive.

◆ KEY ◆

Remember that it's your business and only you will know what direction you want to go in. Even if you find someone else to write your plan you will still have to provide all the information.

KEY POINTS

1. A business plan should explain a company's projected course of action over a period of time, usually the first two to three years after the start-up. In addition, banks, lenders, and other investors will examine the information and financial documentation before deciding whether or not to finance a new business venture.

2. A business plan is an essential tool in obtaining financing and should describe the business itself in detail as well as all important factors influencing the company, including the market, industry, competition, operations and management policies, problem solving strategies, financial resources and needs, and other vital information.

3. A well-written plan will enable the business owner to anticipate costs, plan for difficulties, and take advantage of opportunities, as well as to design and implement strategies that keep the company running as smoothly as possible.

Two business plans are outlined below, the first is for a part time or sole trader start-up and the second for a larger business. Use whichever you feel comfortable with.

BUSINESS PLAN OUTLINES

It is important to write a business plan. The following is a simple format, which will suit a smaller business.

Business Plan 1

Introduction

◆ brief description of the business

◆ business name

- basic details of finance required

- legal structure: sole trader/partnership.

The people

- you: your abilities, skills and experience

- qualifications and relevant work experience

- anyone else involved in the business.

Goals and target

- what you want to get out of the business

- why you are setting the business up

- what targets will measure your progress.

Market research

- why your business will be successful (USP)

- what you know about your customers and competitors

- how you know there is a demand for your product/service.

Practical matters

- insurance

- licences

- health and safety

◆ premises

◆ environment

◆ suppliers.

Finances

◆ what it will cost to get your business started

◆ what the costs of running your business will be

◆ what you will earn

◆ how you will keep your finances under control

◆ one-year cash flow.

You will have realised by now that a lot of the information which is needed for a business plan will have to be estimated or guessed. This is normal. You don't actually know how many shops are going to stock your cards, or how big the electricity bill is going to be, until you start trading. So in the first instance you will have to guess and then alter it as time passes and you can access more accurate figures. For this reason it's a good idea to do the cash flow on a spreadsheet so it can be updated easily.

◆ TIP ◆

Even a simple business plan can be very helpful when making decisions about your business.

Set a time limit to draft out a plan – sometimes the plan becomes more important than the business and this is a mistake. If you are the only person who is going to see it, don't worry about the format just write it so you can understand it.

Business plan 2

The plan below has been provided as a model to help you construct your own in more detail than above. There is no single acceptable format for a business plan, and this example is in no way exclusive, but is intended to serve as a guide.

The main headings included below are topics that should be covered in a comprehensive business plan. They include:

◆ name and type of business

◆ business history and development

◆ description of product or service

◆ market

◆ competition

◆ marketing

◆ operations

◆ administration and management

◆ key personnel

◆ financial information

◆ business strengths and weaknesses and business growth.

Business history and development

Purpose

This section looks at the idea for your business, where it came from, the inspiration behind it and how you intend to develop it taking account of the current market situation.

Includes:

◆ start-up information

◆ owner/key personnel experience

◆ location

◆ development problems and solutions

◆ investment/funding information

◆ future plans and goals

◆ market trends and statistics

◆ major competitors

◆ product/service advantages

◆ national, regional, and local economic impact.

Description of the product or service

This section introduces, defines, and details the product and/or service that will form the basis of your business.

Includes:

◆ USP (unique selling point)*

- niche served

- market comparison

- stage of product/service development

- product/service life cycle

- future growth.

*Your unique selling point is the thing that makes your business different from your competitors. It could be your designs, materials used or level of service. It's important to define this carefully.

Market

This section should give an overview of the market you are entering and where you expect your product or service to fit in.

Includes:

- target market/customer profile

- consumer buying habits

- product/service applications

- test marketing

- market factors and trends

- methods of selling

- pricing.

Competition

Purpose

It is important to know and recognise your competitors. Even if you think yours is a totally new product you will still be competing with others for custom.

Includes:

◆ competitor information

◆ product/service comparison

◆ market niche

◆ product/service strengths and weaknesses

◆ future product/service development.

Marketing

Purpose

Identifies promotion and sales strategies for your product/service.

Includes:

◆ product/service sales appeal

◆ special and unique features

◆ identification of customers

◆ sales and marketing staff

◆ sales cycles

◆ type of advertising/promotion

◆ pricing

◆ competition

◆ customer services.

Operations

Purpose

This section details how your business is run, and traces product/service development from production/inception to the market environment.

Includes:

◆ cost effective production methods

◆ facility

◆ location

◆ equipment

◆ labour

◆ future expansion.

Administration and management

Purpose

Offers a statement of your management philosophy with an in-depth focus on processes and procedures.

Includes:

◆ management philosophy

◆ structure of organisation

◆ reporting system

◆ methods of communication

◆ employee skills and training

◆ employee needs and compensation

◆ work environment

◆ management policies and procedures

◆ roles and responsibilities.

Key personnel

Purpose

Describes the unique backgrounds of principal employees involved in business.

Includes:

◆ owner(s)/employee education and experience

◆ positions and roles

◆ benefits and salary

◆ duties and responsibilities

◆ objectives and goals.

Financial information

Purpose

Finance is at the core of any business. This section should indicate how you are going to finance your business. It will contain detailed financial plans, methods of repayment and future growth opportunities.

Includes:

◆ financial statements

◆ bank loans

◆ methods of repayment

◆ tax returns

◆ start-up costs

◆ projected income (3 years)

◆ projected cash flow (3 years)

◆ projected balance statements (3 years).

Business strengths and weaknesses and business growth

Purpose

Gives an overall view of where the business is now, and where you want it to be in the future.

Includes:

◆ SWOT analysis (strengths, weaknesses, opportunities and threats)

◆ the objectives

◆ plans for future growth.

Appendices

Purpose

Supporting documents used to enhance your business proposal.

Includes:

◆ photographs of product, equipment, facilities, etc.

◆ copyright/trademark documents

◆ legal agreements

◆ marketing materials

◆ research/studies

◆ operation schedules

- organisational charts

- job descriptions

- resumés

- additional financial documentation.

8

Money matters

Keeping control of the money is vital to any business, and the best way to do this is to put some basic systems in place as soon as you start your business. Even if you are working from your kitchen table and selling cards at craft fairs you should treat it as a proper business.

◆ TIP ◆

If you begin keeping records as soon as you start selling you will be able to find out if you are making a profit and covering your costs easily.

Many people who start up in this way treat any sales money as their personal income and so have no money to invest in growing the business. If you intend to grow into a larger business then that is the last thing you should do. To run a business successfully you need to:

◆ know how to finance your business

◆ understand cash flow

◆ control your finances.

HOW TO FINANCE YOUR BUSINESS

All businesses need some capital. You can start small and build up gradually, but it is virtually impossible to start with no money at all. When starting up a business, other people will generally expect you to invest your own money in the venture. This is not unreasonable as it shows you have confidence in your ability to succeed. However, circumstances sometimes dictate that this not possible. If you are leaving university with large student loans, for example, you could find financing a business difficult.

There are several different routes to funding a business so investigate them all when you start up and choose the right one for you. As the business grows you might also need to look again when you require further financing.

Ways of raising finance

◆ your own money

◆ family and friends

◆ bank loan or overdraft

◆ investor

◆ grants

◆ other loans

◆ trade creditors.

Your own money

The cheapest way of starting a business is to use your own money. You can build the business gradually, starting by working at it part time and growing as finance allows. Although this is the most cost effective it might mean that you grow too slowly for the marketplace, and before you can get your ideas into production someone else has used them.

Family and friends

Borrowing from family and friends is a popular way of starting a business but do be careful – if they need their money back in a hurry you could have problems. It's also a good idea to have a contract drawn up about repaying the money, as this will give you some security. If you don't want to go to the expense of a solicitor you can draft a letter and both sign it with a witness; it is doubtful it would stand up in a court of law but it may stop a family dispute from escalating.

Bank loan or overdraft

Borrowing money from a bank is usually an option although they might require security for the loan and the interest rates could be high. A personal loan may work out cheaper than a business loan – so if, for example, you were planning to buy a new car with cash you could consider getting a loan for it and using the cash in the business. For those who have recently left university a graduate loan might be a good idea.

◆ TIP ◆

Any bank will want to be convinced of the viability of the business and will need to see a business plan.

An overdraft is an excellent way of funding everyday cash flow, to tide you over while you are waiting for customers to pay you or to see you through the quiet times of the year. After an initial arrangement fee you only pay interest when you are using the money.

Investor

Anyone who has watched *Dragons' Den* will be aware of the process of involving an investor in your business. Although most investors are not as ruthless as the entrepreneurs involved in this programme, they will want a share of your business in return for investing cash. If you can find an investor who can also offer expertise this could really help your business. You could ask your accountant or business advisor if they know anyone suitable.

Grants

In some areas of the country there are grants available to help you start up your business. They tend to be in the inner city or areas in need of regeneration and you either need to live in them or start your business there. A call to your local enterprise agency or business service should tell you what is available, or you could try typing your postcode into the website www.j4b.co.uk which give business funding advice.

Obtaining a grant, even if they are available, is not always easy. You may have to complete a lot of forms and carry out market research; you also need to check if you have to pay the grant back if you fail to fulfil certain conditions.

Other loans

Specialist organisations who help people set up in business often offer loans. If you are young try the Prince's Trust (this organisation also offers mentors and other support). If you are female and live in the countryside try WIRE (Women in Rural Enterprises).

Avoid at all costs loan companies, which advertise in the paper or on the internet, offering loans with very high interest rates. These are usually easy to obtain, require no security, and can cripple a business.

Trade creditors

If you can persuade your suppliers and printer to give you 30 days credit then this will help with your cash flow. Initial orders, however, will probably have to be paid for immediately so this might only help in the long term.

However you intend to raise the money make sure:

◆ **you calculate how much you need**. A bank or investor will soon spot if you underestimate

◆ **have a proper business plan** and cash flow

◆ work out a survival budget so you know you can still pay the bills while building up the business.

> ◆ TIP ◆
>
> When going to talk to a bank manager or advisor about borrowing money always look smart, know your facts and figures, and have confidence and enthusiasm in your proposal.

Alternative ways of raising the money:

◆ trade down to a small car

◆ increase your mortgage – this is the cheapest way of borrowing money

◆ sell surplus items at car boot sales or on Ebay

◆ take on an extra job and save the income.

OPENING A BUSINESS BANK ACCOUNT

Although many people start a business using their personal account, it doesn't look very professional. It is also very easy to get your money mixed up and stops you building up a credit rating for your business.

With banks competing for your business and offering free banking, if not forever at least for a couple of years, it really is a good idea to open a specific business account. If you are receiving a business loan or grant you may find that they insist on it being paid into a business bank account.

To find a bank first of all investigate what your own bank is offering, and then compare it with at least two others. If you do not need to pay in cash, often an internet bank may prove to be a good choice. Ask other small business people for their recommendations. Some banks provide you with a named business account manager, which you might find helpful.

FINDING AN ACCOUNTANT

Although if you are a sole trader or a partnership you do not need to have an accountant, unless you are very good with figures you will probably find that it will save you money in the long run. Although filling in a tax form is relatively easy, working out what you can and can't claim can be tricky.

Ask friends and other business people for recommendations, make an appointment to see a couple of accountants and go armed with a list of questions (most will see you free of charge for an initial consultation). Ask them if they specialise in small businesses and try and get some idea of their charges – this is not generally easy but the response should give you some idea.

Bookkeepers are not accountants. They merely keep the books and will help you with cash flow. They do not generally prepare accounts for the Inland Revenue.

CASH FLOW

A cash flow forecast is a vital document. It's not difficult to construct, although the first one you do will inevitably consist of some 'guesstimates'. Doing it on the computer is the easiest way to set one up, and it can be updated regularly with a forecast column and an actual column. Most lenders will want to see a 12-month cash flow forecast but to borrow large sums you may need a three-year forecast.

A cash flow lists all the sources of income and outgoings in two sections. The amount of outgoings is subtracted from the income giving you an idea of when and whether you will be making any profit.

Income – the income is all the money you receive from sales of the cards. Don't overestimate this; try and be realistic.

Outgoings – the outgoings are all the expenses/bills you have to pay. These include materials, rent and rates, insurance, telephone, transport, postage and stationery, marketing, wages, bank charges, interest loan repayments, commission to agents and drawings (any money you take out for yourself).

Estimating income

Before you fill in a cash flow you need to estimate the income and outgoings. Income will depend, amongst other things, on the type of cards you are producing. Whilst birthdays do not have a quiet time, Christmas only happens once a year.

Estimating outgoings

Outgoings are harder to estimate during the first year. If you have a friend in a similar business then you can ask them, otherwise you will have to take a calculated guess. Outgoings vary greatly – for example if you are working from home then you will not be paying rent or rates but you will still be using electricity. Marketing costs can be high if you decide to produce a brochure. To calculate your overheads properly you literally have to keep track of everything you spend in connection with the business that is not classed as materials.

> ◆ KEY ◆
>
> Because your cash flow will not be perfect it is important that you monitor it on a monthly basis to make sure your outgoings are not exceeding your income, or that if they are you have sufficient cash to cover it.

Profit and loss account

From your cash flow you can construct a profit and loss account. This shows what has happened in your business in terms of income, sales and expenditure over a given period.

Break even point

Once you have estimated how many cards you could sell you need to work out how many you need to sell to make a profit. This figure may surprise you – people generally underestimate the level of sales they need to keep going.

It is good to set yourself targets; no one expects a business to make money from day one but you need to know that you are going in the right direction.

CONTROLLING YOUR FINANCES

You need to keep clear records of your:

◆ credit

◆ stock

◆ cash.

You can either do it on a computer or by keeping manual books; use whatever method is comfortable for you. They need to be done regularly and if you find them difficult you will put it off.

Bookkeeping

This is the term used for the systems which keep financial control of your business. When you are starting up you might find it easiest to buy an accounting book such as Simplex D or Everite, or you could use a computer accounts program such as Quicken or Sage. Check with your accountant (if you are using one) as they may have a preferred system.

As well as filling in the book or spreadsheet regularly you need to keep all receipts and invoices. Large lever arch files are good for this: file them in date order month by month so you or your accountant can find them easily at the end of the year. If you have a lot of small receipts attach them to A4 sheets to stop them getting lost. You don't want to pay any more tax than you have to!

Invoices

If you are supplying shops or galleries you will be expected to invoice them. Set up an invoice system so you know when your payment is due.

Statements

Statements are usually sent 30 days after the invoice if payment is not received. Sending invoices and statements regularly, as soon as they are due, is the key to good money management.

Credit

The normal amount of credit expected by retailers is 30 days although the larger multiples can expect between three to six months! If you are having your cards handled by a distribution service you might have to wait considerably longer and you will need extra capital to see you through this period.

Sale or return

Sale or return is one of the bugbears of the industry. If you are just starting out many retailers will offer to take your cards on sale or return. This is reasonable for a first order, but once you have proved that your cards will sell then they should be prepared to buy them. Some local authority and charity outlets don't have money for stock so if you want to supply them you may have to do it this way.

> ◆ TIP ◆
>
> If you supply on sale or return keep records carefully and invoice on a monthly basis for what has been sold.

Some large retailing chains have now also started demanding cards on sale or return. If they are taking large quantities and returning a lot of the stock this could lead you into a financial quagmire. It might be great to see your cards on sale in a major retailer in the town centre, but don't let yourself get carried away by this if the figures don't add up.

Chasing payment

If you have not been paid on time and have sent a statement with no response, then make a polite telephone call to remind them. If this doesn't have any effect keep sending reminders, followed up with a telephone call. Some large companies automatically wait 60 days or until the statement arrives so try and find out what date payments are made and who is responsible. Persistence usually pays off – some firms are just slow payers.

> ◆ TIP ◆
>
> Don't send any further stock until the first delivery has been paid for.

Top tips for getting paid

◆ If you are not good at keeping on top of creditors hire someone to do it. Paying for someone to work a day a month to keep on top of cash flow can be money well spent.

◆ Don't automatically give credit. Check references carefully and make a considered judgement. Giving credit is like lending money so be careful.

◆ If it's a large order try invoicing and delivering in stages.

◆ Consider using discounting/factoring, this involves signing over all your invoices to someone (usually a bank) for them to collect. They pay you part of the invoice immediately and then the balance, minus their commission, when they collect.

◆ If you expect other people to pay you on time then remember to do likewise.

PENSIONS

In an ideal world we would all have a pension plan and it would perform properly. Whatever you think about pensions one thing is true – the sooner you start saving towards your retirement the better. If you don't think you can afford a pension at present then try and put a regular sum away and review the situation annually.

The most efficient way of doing this for most people is by having an ISA. The individual savings account was launched by the government to encourage people to save for the future. It is a tax-efficient way of saving money and can be either stock-market investments or a traditional saving account. As an incentive, any interest earned from money held in an ISA is tax free. Therefore it is a good way of building up savings towards your pension. There is a limit as to how much you can hold in an ISA (currently this is £7,200).

◆ TIP ◆

If you intend to start a pension then discuss this with your accountant or take advice from at least two independent financial advisors.

9

Pricing and paperwork

PRICING

Pricing your cards correctly can make the difference between building a successful business and giving money away. Getting the price right is really important: a 10 per cent increase in price can increase profitability by 40 per cent and vice versa. The right price is the one the customer is prepared to pay. Providing this allows you to make a profit, you are in business.

There are various ways of calculating how much it costs to produce a card. This will give you an indication of how much you can charge and make a profit. Because the industry has a fairly fixed pricing structure you will have to operate within that in order to compete. The simplest way to work out the prices is to make a batch of, for instance, 10 cards, and then calculate the costs. That is the materials used and your time. You also need to allow for overheads – to simplify this when you start in business add 10p to each card.

To produce 10 handmade cards

Materials (including envelopes/cello wrap etc.)	£4.00
Time (1 hour@£10 per hour)	£10.00
Overheads	£1.00
Total	£15.00

This means that each card costs £1.50 to make; you therefore need to sell them for more than this in order to make a profit. By comparing your cards with others on the market you might be able to work out how much you can reasonably sell them for. Hopefully it is more than £1.50 – if not then you need to took at the design or the time taken and see if you can reduce the costs.

This is a very simple example. There are many ways of calculating prices but you always need to remember to include materials, time and overheads in your pricing and then add a profit margin. This will allow for cards that don't sell and enable you to purchase new equipment and so on.

◆ TIP ◆

If you intend to sell your cards via retailers, remember they will multiply the wholesale price by 2.35 to achieve the retail price.

People's expectations of what they are prepared to pay for a card are fixed. For instance, no one has yet tried to sell a £20 card in an ordinary range. You could try, but unless you are producing something very special you are unlikely to succeed because this will be above the price that people are prepared to pay. At the opposite end of the scale cheapness does not necessarily mean good value, and purchasing a cheap card may not give the customer satisfaction.

Entering the market

Taking care to price correctly as you enter the market is important. Once you are known as a supplier of cheap cards it would be difficult to move to the more lucrative upmarket sector, so position your cards carefully.

The type of card you are producing will affect your pricing strategy. However all the basic costs will be the same, so in order to make a profit you need to ensure that the following are included:

◆ labour

◆ materials

◆ equipment

◆ marketing

◆ overheads.

The method of pricing cards will vary depending on whether you are producing handmade or art cards or a published range. These are general guidelines as to what you should include:

Labour

This will include your time and that of any employees involved in producing the card. If you are hand making cards you can work out quite easily how long it takes you to produce each card. But what you also need to remember with any type of card is the amount of time you spend at suppliers, with printers, and marketing your product.

◆ TIP ◆

To work out the time to produce cards, always make a batch. Making individual cards will take more time and the more you make the speedier you should become.

Materials

Material costs include the card, cello wrap, any embellishments, glues etc. If the cards are being printed you will find it easier to calculate these costs, as the printer will quote you a price for a certain quantity.

Equipment

There is some sophisticated and sometimes expensive equipment available to help with making handmade cards. This includes printers, computers, trimmers, laminating machines, etc. These items will have a limited life span and have to be replaced. To allow for this you need to include them in your costings (see example below). If you are having the cards professionally printed you do not need to include the printer's machinery, as this is part of their overheads.

Marketing

Under this heading you could include the commission you pay the agents, and the rent at craft fairs or trade exhibitions. You should also include publicity material, and any advertising you intend to do.

Overheads

The overheads include everything else – they are all the expenses involved in running a business apart from your time and the materials – such as travel, phone, rent and rates, electricity, and insurance. It is quite difficult to work out the overheads when you are setting up but when you have completed a year in business it becomes easier. You can add up all your bills, divide by 52, and you will know what it costs to run your business for a week. You will also know how many cards you can produce and sell within a week; if you divide this into the cost of the overheads then you will know how much to add on.

Pricing handmade cards

Pricing handmade cards can be quite difficult. You definitely want to price your cards to make a good profit but how much should you charge and what percentage should you add for profit?

Handmade cards are, by their nature, time-consuming. Materials can be cheap but allowing for all the labour can push costs up considerably. Timing how long it takes you to make a card is vital.

One maker had to rethink her ideas when she discovered that it took her eight hours to make five cards. Although they were very ornate and would have commanded a premium price they still did not provide the foundation for a business. If this happens to you don't let it put you off – use your creative skills to redesign the cards so they take less time, or source other materials which reduce the time taken.

KEY ◆

With more practice and experience you will find that you are able to accomplish more in less time.

Pricing example for handmade cards

Producing 1,000 cards per month (several designs but all taking roughly the same time)

Labour 100 hours @ £7.50 per hour	£750
Materials	£300

Tools
To include any expenditure you want to write
off e.g. a printer costing £200 will last 3 years
£200 ÷ 36 =   £5.55 per month

Overheads
When you are starting up you will probably
work from home and have low overheads try
allowing   £50 per month

Marketing
Rent at fairs will be the largest cost
and could amount to   £100 per month

TOTAL   £1,205.55

This will give you a total cost for 1,000 cards of £1,205 – i.e. each card costs £1.20 to produce.

If you then sell them at craft fairs for £2.95 you are making a good profit. On the other hand, if you sell them to shops for £1.50 for them to sell on at £3.50 you will have to sell an awful lot of cards to generate a viable business.

Pricing printed cards

With printed cards you are entering the mass market where quantity rules. The cost of producing these cards may seem very cheap but bear in mind that you may not sell them all and will therefore have quite a lot of wastage.

To assess what price shops are paying to card manufacturers remember that they will almost certainly be putting on a mark up of 235–300 per cent. This means that if the shop sells the card at £2.50 they will have paid approx £1. From this you will see that printed cards selling at £1.25 will have cost the retailer about 50p.

The large chains are notorious for forcing down prices from small manufacturers and offers of 10p a card are not unknown. You have been warned. One way to overcome this is to produce cards with a higher value or an element of difference, which the consumer will pay extra for. Target independent retailers looking for something unusual and you could be on to a winner.

◆ KEY ◆

Remember that although printed cards are cheaper to produce you will have to sell large quantities to make it financially viable. This will probably include employing agents and their commission will need to be included in your pricing.

UNDERSTANDING THE CARD MARKET

As well as calculating the finances it is important to understand the way the card market works. Here are some tips.

◆ The retail price is the price the customer pays for your card.

◆ The wholesale price is the price the retailer pays for your card.

◆ The RSP is the price you can recommend retailers sell your cards at, but you cannot enforce this.

◆ Reducing card prices does not necessarily increase sales.

◆ If you find that your cards are flying out and you cannot keep up with production then you have probably under priced them.

◆ Retailers may expect exclusivity from card companies, i.e. they may insist that they are the only stockists within a given area. This can be difficult to enforce if you are supplying small chains.

◆ Most retailers will expect the cards to be supplied carriage paid, and this cost will need to be allowed for when pricing.

Sale or return

If you are supplying on sale or return, different rules apply.

◆ The retailer should expect a smaller percentage e.g. 30–40 per cent of the retail price, as they are not risking their money.

◆ Damaged stock: even with cello-wrapped cards some damaged cards are inevitable. Generally you will be expected to fund these.

◆ If cards are shoplifted the retailer should still pay you.

◆ It is up to you to keep a close watch on stock levels and send invoices when appropriate.

◆ You may find it useful to supply a spinner or display stand and to insist that this is used solely for your cards.

As a compromise, to encourage a retailer to stock your cards you could offer for the initial order to exchange cards that have been slow sellers. Retailers are often reluctant to try new ranges so this is a good way to get a foot in the door.

PAPERWORK

In order to sell cards to retailers you need to set up a system of invoicing, delivery notes and statements. Keeping this paperwork up to date is important. If you set templates up on the computer when you begin then it is easy to keep it up on a regular basis.

You should set the following templates up on your computer so you can despatch them easily:

♦ order form

♦ delivery note

♦ invoice

♦ statement.

Order form

Whether you are taking orders from a trade fair or from visiting a shop you need to take the orders down professionally and ask the retailer to sign the document. You can either print some order forms or you can use an order book. If you use order forms clip them on to a board and send a copy to the retailer when you return; with an order book you can generally give them a copy when they place the order. If you are printing your own include the terms of trading or have these available separately.

Delivery note

You should always pack a delivery note in with an order when sending by carrier and send the invoice separately. Most retailers prefer this, and if the invoice arrives and the goods don't they can contact you.

> **◆ TIP ◆**
>
> Some retailers do not like their staff to know how much stock costs, so do not put the prices on the delivery note.

Invoice

An invoice is sent when you despatch the goods. This should include details of your terms of trading (see below). If you have asked the retailer to pay before delivery then you should send a pro-forma invoice and once you have received payment despatch the goods. (A pro-forma invoice is one issued when the goods are ready for despatch but haven't been sent.)

Statement

It is normal to send out a statement to your customers to remind them to pay. You can send all your statements out on a fixed day each month, or you can send them 30 days from the day of invoice – whatever suits you best. But don't miss out on sending statements; many businesses don't pay until they receive them.

If you can find out when a business pays the cheques you can make sure your paperwork is in then, otherwise you might have to wait a month.

TERMS OF TRADING

When customers order from you they will want to know what the terms and conditions are. These are known as terms of trading and are usually printed on order forms and invoices. Most card companies will have similar terms of trading and they all include the following information.

Ordering

How orders can be placed e.g. telephone, fax, internet, with agents etc. Size of orders, if there is a minimum order.

Prices

Information that refers to your pricing structure: does it include VAT, is there a discount for quantity? etc.

New customers

Do new customers have to pay by pro-forma? Also the type of references you require to set up a credit account.

Accounts and late payment

Details of your credit terms (generally 30 days). What happens if the customer fails to pay: will they be referred to a debt agency, will you charge interest?

You can also include the following words:

'In addition we reserve the right to charge interest and compensation for debt recovery costs which could be charged on overdue invoices using the entitlements provided by the "Amended late Payment of Commercial Debts (Interest) Act 1998" and the "Late Payment of Commercial debts Regulations 2002".'

◆ KEY ◆

In reality this sanction is rarely used, as the intention is to build a good working relationship with your customers.

Payments

How you accept payment. This could be by cheque (if so name the payee), by banker's transfer, or credit card.

Carriage paid

Free carriage is normal for orders of a certain level. It is a good idea to package some cards and find out how much it will cost to post them – this should give you an idea of how large the order needs to be in order for you to pay carriage.

Carriage costs

Orders under the amount above are either charged at a fixed rate or at cost. These figures might vary if you are sending cards abroad.

Damaged goods and returns

You should state how long the retailer has to return any damaged goods (this is generally seven days), or at least to notify you within seven days and the agent will collect on their next visit.

Title claim

In order to protect yourself against retailers who go out of business the following words are generally inserted in the terms of trading:

'These goods remain the property of _____ (insert your name) until such time as they are paid for. The risk in the goods shall pass to the buyer on delivery but the ownership of the goods shall remain with _____ until full payment has been received from the buyer.'

It is also a good idea to include the following:

'All designs supplied are original designs by _____ and are protected by copyright. In the event of any unauthorised copying _____ are entitled to take legal proceedings against the customer, wholesaler or manufacturer.'

◆ TIP ◆

If you belong to an anti-copying organisation their logo should be shown on all the above forms.

10

Marketing

Whatever type of card business you're in it's important to consider your customers. Most people buy cards, but different groups of people buy different types of card. Students may buy funny cards, for example, the elderly may prefer verses.

When producing a range of cards, spend time considering who will buy them, and therefore where you will sell them. It is time well spent. If you are selling via retailers you have in effect two customers – the retailer and the actual customer who buys and sends the card.

In order to do your marketing properly you need to work through it in stages:

1. identify your customer

2. carry out some market research

3. research your competitors

4. do some test trading

5. prepare a marketing plan.

IDENTIFYING YOUR CUSTOMER

The majority of your customers are likely to be individuals looking for cards for special or seasonal occasions. With the exception of Valentine's Day, when a lot of men buy cards, most of your customers will be women.

Many people buy cards in advance or in bulk, particularly if they have a favourite card shop or like one range of cards. These are the type of customers you want, the ones who really like your cards and will travel to a specific shop or craft fair to buy them. The other type of customers are the ones who, when they need a card, just pop into their local shop.

◆ KEY ◆

When designing it will help if you have a customer in mind. If you have no clear idea then doing some research is a good idea.

Most people start by making the cards and then trying to sell them, often not even thinking about the business potential. This is a good way of testing the market. If your family and friends buy your cards then maybe someone else will. It doesn't follow that if your family and friends do buy your cards that you have a potential business as they might be doing it out of kindness.

Ask yourself the question: Who will buy my cards?

You may think that you know the answer to this question but you need to prove your instinct by carrying out some market research.

MARKET RESEARCH

Market research is the method by which you find out if there is a market for your cards before you go to the expense of having a range published or produce large quantities of cards. You can do this in a variety of ways, such as:

◆ questionnaire/survey of consumers

◆ taking a stand at a craft fair

◆ visiting card shops and showing the buyers your cards.

Although it is a good idea to carry out some market research and therefore minimise the risk, it is by no means foolproof – tastes change and by the time you have your cards on sale they may no longer be fashionable.

Consumer survey

By all means ask friends and family, but also ask other people who will give you an objective opinion. You can do this by standing in a shopping centre and showing people samples of your cards, and asking them to rate them on a scale of 1–5. You can also ask questions such as:

1. How often do you buy cards?

2. How much do you usually pay?

3. Do you buy from any particular shops?

4. Do you choose any special brands?

5. If so, which ones?

6. Do you like this card (show sample)?

7. Would you buy it?

8. How much would you expect to pay for it?

9. Are there any cards you would like but find it difficult to buy?

10. Do you like verses?

Practise this technique on friends; people don't want to spend a lot of time answering questions, so work on a slick presentation.

◆ TIP ◆

Try and focus on people who send a lot of cards. It's not a lot of use if the people who like your cards only send one a year to their mum!

Taking a stand at a craft fair

If you are making handmade cards, trying them out at a craft fair can be a good test of their saleability. However although the cards might sell to people in this environment they won't necessarily sell in a card shop.

Keep a clipboard handy and jot down people's comments. Don't forget to have a good look at the other stalls selling cards and see who is buying from them. If you have a poor position at a craft fair this may affect your sales so don't be too dispirited if you have a bad day – it may still be worth having another go or trying some other market research.

Visiting card shops

As part of your research ask local shopkeepers for their opinion. Compose a short questionnaire and take it to a number of retailers with the cards. Write down the answers. That way you can judge whether the responses are all the same.

Most people will find you some time if you explain what you are doing and avoid busy periods. Questions you can ask include:

1. Which is your best-selling card?

2. Which is the most popular range?

3. Are there any types of cards you find it difficult to obtain?

4. Do photographic/art/handmade cards sell well in your shop?

5. Do you prefer to have stands supplied by the card company?

6. Where do you buy your cards? e.g. trade fair

7. Do you like these cards?

8. Do you think they would sell in your shop?

9. The price range is £x–y: do you think that would be acceptable?

10. Would you consider stocking them?

Questions 8 and 10 may seem similar, but the retailer may like the cards and think they would sell but have no room. In that case it might be worth a repeat visit when they are looking for a new range.

♦ TIP ♦

When carrying out your market research remember that women buy 85 per cent of cards, and that birthdays are the most popular occasion.

Your cards need a reason for someone to buy them, for instance a birthday, new baby or other special occasions. Ranges that have amusing slogans but no direct purpose can be successful but you will need to find outlets where the customers buy this type of card.

You also need to research the cards already on the market thoroughly. There is no point copying other people's ideas – to be a success you will have to come up with something original.

Researching the existing market

You can research the market in several different ways, but do it professionally. Gather as much information as you can and then use it to make decisions about the type of cards to produce and where to sell them.

Visit card shops

Visit your local card shops and others further afield and buy samples of cards similar to those you intend to produce. You can then compare them for quality and price. Look at the envelopes used, the printing on the back, the information provided, how they are packaged etc. Remember that most retailers will add 135% to the price of a card that is 100% profit +VAT. This means that if you buy a card for £2.35 the retailer has paid £1. In some more expensive areas the mark up could be as much as 300 per cent so take this into account when working out the price of your cards.

Research the internet

There is a lot of information available on the internet. A list of useful websites is given at the end of the book; one of the main websites is the GCA. Also look at the sites of the big card companies such as Paper House, Medici, Woodmansterne and Hallmark.

Trade shows

It is a good idea to visit a trade show as soon as possible. The Spring Fair in February at the Birmingham NEC is widely recognised as the most important fair for greeting cards companies. All the big companies exhibit there and there is also a section for smaller design-led companies.

If you want to sell your designs then go towards the end of the show and take a small portfolio. Approach the people on the stands, say that you are a card designer, and ask how you should contact their company. They should give you the names of the people to contact.

◆ TIP ◆

Read the chapter on Copyright and Licensing Agreements before handing anything over.

A smaller trade show where many handmade card companies start out is the BCTF (British Craft Trade Fair) in Harrogate. Held in April it attracts a lot of gallery buyers and can be a useful place to exhibit, as you will learn a lot from talking to the other stallholders.

Having learnt as much as you can about the market, re-look at your designs and ideas for the business and ask yourself the following:

◆ Who will be the purchaser or recipient?

◆ Which retailers will stock your cards?

THE COMPETITION

While researching the existing market and the opportunities available you will also gain some information about the competition. This will be very useful as you also need to research the cards already on the market thoroughly. There is no point copying other people's ideas – to be a success you will have to come up with something original.

Spending some time in card shops and watching the type of people who select a particular card can be useful. Also visit areas you wouldn't normally go to: if you usually shop in shopping centres, visit villages and town centres. Remember that to make a success of your business you will have to sell a lot of cards and this will mean having as many stockists as possible. Identifying where these stockists are will be useful information.

Who are your competitors

When starting any business you must remember that you will have a number of competitors; the card market is no exception.

◆ There are approximately 800 card publishers serving the UK market. These range from small-scale traders to large national and international companies.

◆ Some companies have their own retail outlets. These large organisations tend to dominate the market and can be found on every high street in the UK, providing economies of scale with which small companies can't hope to compete.

◆ If you become too popular you may find yourself the target of people who may wish to buy you out. You may also find yourself the victim of copying.

◆ The internet provides a newer and growing type of competition. Online greeting services are becoming increasingly popular and companies such as Moon Pig are making a substantial dent in the market.

◆ Charity cards are also a major competitor and one charity has recently opened its own chain of card shops. Particularly at Christmas charity cards take a large share of the market.

◆ TIP ◆

Working out how you are going to compete with your competitors is part of the marketing process.

TEST TRADING

Test marketing (or test trading) is when you try and trade in a limited way to see if your cards will sell. This can be difficult in the card market as retailers are unlikely to take a few to see if they sell. Also, if you are selling printed cards, you will have had to invest some money in a print run in order to test trade. Sometimes in business you have to go with your instincts, but if you can carry out some test marketing it could save you from making costly mistakes.

Before testing the market you need to decide

Who will be the purchaser/recipient – if you are designing cards for students, for example, then they need to be sold in outlets frequented by students. You will need to test market in these areas, i.e. university towns, not areas with a predominantly elderly population.

Which retailers will stock your cards – visit as many retailers as you can informally and find ones that stock your type of cards. These are the ones you should approach.

The next step is to visit retailers, explain that you are setting up a business and would like their advice. Go when the shop is quiet and if the owner/buyer isn't there be prepared to talk to the assistant – they will know their customers.

◆ Ensure samples are labelled properly and are properly presented. Tatty samples or ones printed poorly will not attract positive comments. The excuse that these are only samples and that the real ones will be better cuts no ice with buyers.

◆ When test trading it's a good idea to have a few questions written down so that you ask everyone the same questions and therefore can easily evaluate the response (see the earlier section on visiting card shops).

◆ Don't argue – if they don't like the cards or say that they are not for them, just ask if they can suggest anywhere else you might try.

PREPARE A MARKETING PLAN

There are two important things to remember when marketing.

The first is the rule of the four Ps; the second is the rule of four.

The four Ps

◆ Product

◆ Place

◆ Price

◆ Promote

Basically this means having the right *product* in the right *place* at the right *price* and *promoting* it properly. If you have done your market research properly you should know where the right place is to promote your product, you should have also worked out the correct pricing structure. Presuming you have a great product it's all systems go!

The rule of four

The rule of four (also known as the AIDA theory) is about the way people make purchases.

The first time someone sees your cards they become *aware* of them.

The second time they become *interested*.

The third time they might actually *desire* your cards, but it's only on the fourth time that they take *action* and buy the card.

◆ KEY ◆

80 per cent of sales come after the fourth contact that is made.

From this you can see that just exhibiting your cards at one craft fair is unlikely to be successful. However you can increase your chances of success by advertising in the fair brochure, sending out information to potential retailers, and producing a flier.

Over time people will begin to see your cards; the first time may be in a shop, the second time someone might send them one, the third time might be something in the press about your range. The fourth time they see them hopefully they will buy them.

Advertising

Unless you are opening a shop you are unlikely to go down traditional advertising routes. As a small card producer you will benefit from the advertising carried out by large retailers. One year ASDA mounted a very expensive Valentine's Day campaign and sales soared throughout the industry. Promoting your cards will be done more directly via mailshots, trade fairs and agents. You might want to consider advertising in the trade press particularly to help you get started but be careful with your budget – advertising people are very good at getting you to spend a lot of money!

11

Presentation, packaging and display

Good presentation and packaging is crucial to most products, and vital to greeting cards. The wrong envelope, poor quality cello wrap (which attracts dust), and inadequate labelling, can all mean lost sales. A cheap envelope with a quality card can not only spoil the appearance of the product but also reduce the value.

Research is important: always write on and post envelopes that you intend to use to avoid costly mistakes. One large company once issued silver envelopes which were impossible to write on. They had to withdraw a whole range of Christmas cards – mistakes can be expensive.

◆ TIP ◆

Coloured envelopes are popular but if they are too dark you can't see the writing.

ENVELOPES

Pre-folded cards generally come with envelopes but if you are making your own cards or having them printed then you will need to buy some. Your printer may supply envelopes or you can buy from a supplier (see Fact File).

Special envelopes

In addition to normal envelopes you can buy small boxes or 'deep envelopes' with added depth for cards which have a lot of embellishment (see 'Boxed cards' below). You can also be very creative and use CD covers as envelopes or make your own. The easiest way to do this is to use a commercial envelope as a template, open it up and draw round it.

Ordering envelopes

There are four main types of envelopes:

C6	114 mm × 162 mm
Square	130 mm × 130 mm
5 × 7	125 mm × 175 mm
Slim	available in various sizes.

It makes sense to produce cards in these sizes as these envelopes are produced in large quantities and therefore more cost effective. It also means that they will fit easily into card fittings. As with most things, the larger the quantity you buy the cheaper the envelopes, so using one size will work out cheaper than using small quantities of different sizes. They are all available in a wide variety of different papers.

A good fit

Make sure that the card will fit into the envelope. The standard tolerance is 5 mm but if your card is quite bulky with added decoration then you may need it to be larger.

Boxed cards

Some cards, such as decoupage cards, will need to be posted in boxes. Boxes are available from specialist suppliers but are expensive. Always test your card's ability to stand up to the postal system by posting one to yourself! If you are using fragile items on the cards, check whether they will go through the post or if they need a special envelope.

THE POST

Also consider the postal system in some countries (including the UK): both size and depth is considered when pricing the stamp. Rates of postage vary and this will add to the customer's cost and might be important to the customer – particularly at the lower end of the market.

LABELLING

Remember to label your cards with your name and a contact number or website address. This is particularly important if you are planning to sell all the cards yourself – if people like your cards they need to know where they can get more of them. Next time the order might be for 30 Christmas cards or 50 wedding invitations.

Methods of labelling

There are several methods of labelling cards. The ideal way is to have the cards printed but this is only worth doing when you are producing in quantity. In the meantime, try one of the following:

◆ **Adhesive labels** – these can be printed with your name, contact details and logo. They are available in silver and gold as well as transparent. You attach them to the back of the card. You can make them yourself or purchase them from a firm such as www.stickylabels.co.uk.

◆ **Stamping** – you can have a stamp made with your name on and, using an ink pad, stamp the back of each card.

◆ **Computer** – if the cards you are using will go through the printer you can print your details on the cards that way.

◆ TIP ◆

Remember to place labels on the card – you can label the cello wrap envelope as well but it will be thrown away.

CELLO WRAPPING

If you decide to use a cello bag, and this will depend on where you intend to sell your cards, you will have to make some decisions. There are two main types of bag: OPP (oriented polypropylene) and CPP (cast poly-propylene). The main difference is that OPP is high gloss, high clarity film which gives extra sparkle and therefore makes the cards look more attractive. It is the one most often used by the major card companies. CPP is a stronger film with better slip characteristics.

You should always buy good quality bags – the small difference in price is well worth the extra, particularly with handmade cards.

◆ TIP ◆

Some bags seem to attract dust more than others so it's worth testing before you buy in quantity.

Initially you can buy small packs of cello bags from hobby shops and mail order stockists, but there is a huge saving when you start to buy by the thousand. When you feel ready to purchase in bulk, check the suppliers' list at the back of the book, contact them and ask for a sample.

◆ TIP ◆

Cards on uncoated stock which soils easily are often avoided by buyers unless cello-wrapped.

Sizes

Standard bags are widely available for standard cards, e.g. 7×5. In order to keep ahead of the market large firms often bring out unusual sized cards, but don't expect their cello wrap to be immediately available and having them made especially for you will be expensive.

There are various types: some bags have a flap, some are self-adhesive and some are designed to be sealed with a sticker. If you need the customer to read the inside of the card you will have to use large bags, which open up.

Branding

Bags can be branded with your logo but you would need to order huge quantities to make it viable. You can use a sticker with your details on but bear in mind that if you are supplying shops they may prefer you just to put your name on – they won't want to advertise your company but their own.

Having the cards professionally wrapped

Most cards, particularly handmade cards, will need to be cello wrapped. Initially you will probably do this yourself, but if you start to produce large quantities you may want to use a specialist firm. This can be cost effective but remember to instruct them to check the cards and discard ones which are faulty, e.g. with smudges etc. Some spoiled cards are inevitable in a print run but it won't make your customers happy if you include them in an order. (The supply of faulty cards is officially called setoff, and the printer usually allows for this by printing extra cards.)

◆ TIP ◆

If you are going to have your cards packed by a card packing firm they will provide the bags.

Banding

Once wrapped they need to be banded in sixes or twelves, then boxed with a delivery note and other necessary information. It is advisable to send the invoice separately so that if the parcel doesn't arrive the retailer will contact you.

PACKING FOR DELIVERY

Make sure that the box you use is strong enough, and include adequate packing material. Enclose the right paperwork (see Chapter 9). If it is a small order resist the temptation to use a padded envelope as the cards will almost certainly end up bent. Samples can be sent in these if you encase the cards in thick cardboard.

If you want to use elastic bands make sure that they are not going to kink the cards; an alternative is a cardboard strip fixed with a piece of sellotape.

POINT OF SALE

Most retailers appreciate point of sale material to help promote your product. If you are an artist or making handmade cards they may want some information about you and perhaps a photo. Alternatively you could produce a new range and have some display boards made to promote this. You could have one of the card designs blown up and made into a poster.

DISPLAYING CARDS

If you are selling the cards yourself at a trade fair or exhibition you will need to display them properly. Portable card stands are available in acrylic, card or wire depending on the look and the market you are aiming for. Even at a craft fair spending some money on decent stands can pay dividends.

To source the stands look for shop fittings' suppliers in the *Yellow Pages* or do an internet search. If you are supplying shops you may want to take into account the type of stands they use, or even supply them on loan. Some retailers will ask for sample cards to use for window display; you can send these with or without envelopes.

Card stands

There are many types of display stand available and they come in a variety of sizes and shapes: cardboard, acrylic, wire, wooden.

Cardboard stands

These are the cheapest form of stands. They generally come flat-packed and are easy to put together, but unfortunately they soon start to look tatty so if you intend to exhibit at a lot of fairs it is probably worth investing in something more substantial.

Acrylic stands

These vary in size from single stands that display one card to portable stands displaying a range on a counter. They also include stands which will fit into the slat boards used by the majority of shop fitters.

Wire stands

Wire stands generally stand on the floor. They can hold a large number of different cards and sometimes different sizes. They are relatively cheap to buy in stock sizes and many card companies supply them on loan free of charge. If you produce unusually shaped cards you may have to have this type of stand custom made, which can be very expensive and is not as versatile.

Wooden stands

Most card shops have wooden stands as they are the most cost-effective way of displaying a large number of cards. They have between 9 and 15 rows of cards so if you are supplying shops remember that they may want a large number to make a decent display.

It is a good idea to consider how you are going to display your cards when you are designing their size and shape.

Other display items

Picture frames

Large picture frames can be used at fairs to display cards; remove the glass and paint the hardboard or cover with fabric. Hung on the backing boards round a stand these can look very impressive for little cost. A more contemporary look can be achieved using Perspex panels.

Washing lines

Most craft shops sell small silver and gold pegs which can be used to peg cards onto fancy string; these make interesting displays and help move the customer's eye around the stand.

Apply your creativity to designing your display and it will give an edge by attracting people to your stand.

12

Getting publicity

WHAT IS PUBLIC RELATIONS?

In a media-obsessed society it is important to consider how you are going to promote your business. Doing this properly will help you to communicate with your customers and others who are crucial to the success of your business.

The method by which businesses publicise themselves in the media is known as public relations; it works by using the media to build your image, to introduce new customers to your products and to tell people what you are doing with your business – whether this is launching a new range of cards or winning an award.

Who do I need to communicate with?

The people you need to communicate with are all those who can influence your business and help you to make it a success. This can include more people than you imagine. Obviously your customers are one sector, whether these are retailers or the general public, it also includes your bank manager, suppliers, accountants, and even your friends and relations.

If you are a designer your public might include card companies as well as the general public who buy your cards, your competitors and your business advisors. If you are making and selling your own cards to retailers they will also be your public.

Public relations is simply about building a relationship with the press, learning to write a press release and promoting your business in the media at every opportunity.

Many people misunderstand the nature of public relations thinking of it as free advertising. In fact it is anything but. For public relations to work for your business you need to devote a lot of time to it. As this is your time then it naturally 'costs' money, although the cost may be hidden. If you don't want to do this yourself you can employ a PR agency but unless you are starting a large-scale business this will be an unnecessary expense.

How does it work?

When people read about your products in the press it could have an effect on your business. For instance, if you have your cards featured in an upmarket consumer magazine this can encourage quality shops to stock them.

Winning an award such as one of the Henries* with the resulting publicity can transform your business as consumers hear about your cards and start asking for them leading to increased sales.

HOW TO CONTACT THE PRESS

The standard way of contacting the press is by sending out a press release. These are easy to write but should follow a certain format to look professional.

---

*The Henries are the greeting card industry's Oscars. Held annually they are organised by *Progressive Greetings* and have many different categories including one for handmade cards.

> ◆ TIP ◆
>
> Remember that journalists get scores of press releases every day and what they are looking for is a good story.

Good stories in their eyes generally have a human interest angle, so although you may want to wax lyrical about your cards they are just as likely to want information about you.

When you send out a press release any journalist that is interested in the story will contact you for more information. You don't have to put every detail in the press release, in fact if you do it will be to your disadvantage as the journalist won't have enough time to read it.

Most journalists use Mac computers so make sure anything you send is compatible. This is important as they work to very tight deadlines and don't have time to retype your press release.

Disadvantages

It is not free advertising – you have no control over if, or when, anything will appear in the press. So if you were opening a shop or attending a fair and hoped to gain publicity on a specific day then an advertisement might be better.

Advantages

People tend to believe what they read in the editorial section more than in the adverts. It is a very cost-effective way of reaching your customer; even a small mention in a publication can reach a huge number of people at less cost than an advertisement.

What type of story appeals to the press?

The press release should focus on what you and your business are doing; the media particularly likes human interest stories so think about the personal angle. Types of stories that work well are about

◆ opening new premises

◆ launch of a new range

◆ winning an award

◆ supplying to a celebrity.

Remember that not every story will appeal to every publication. Opening a new card shop may appeal to the local press, winning an award may make a good story for the local radio and supplying cards for a celebrity wedding might interest the trade press.

PRESS RELEASES

What is a press release?

A press release is an easy way for a business to tell the media about products, events and interesting developments. It is also the most effective way of attracting media interest.

Why are they used?

They are the simplest and quickest way of getting a story to the journalist or researcher working in the media. A well-written press release will look professional and present your information to the busy journalist as quickly as possible.

Rules for writing a press release

1. A press release is the standard way of getting information to the media. As such it should always be **interesting**, **topical** and **newsworthy**.

2. It should answer the questions **Why? What? Where? When?** and **Who?** This is vital information and can be easily overlooked.

3. A **good headline** will attract attention, but don't try and be too clever – you are not the journalist. Try and use at least one of the following attention – grabbing words: **new, first, success**.

4. Always include an **image** – postcard or photograph for a mailshot, Jpeg file for email. This will have an immediate impact.

5. One or two **quotes** are always useful, one from yourself and one from a respected professional or satisfied customer, preferably with a public profile.

6. **Don't make it too long.** One sheet of A4 should be enough to get your message across and then if the journalist is interested they will contact you.

7. Always write in the proper format so it looks **professional**. A free gift i.e. a card is always appreciated but won't guarantee publication!

8. **Never fold** a press release – use large envelopes for mail shots. Use headed or coloured paper to make it stand out.

9. When sending by email editors prefer you to cut and paste rather than use attachments. It saves them time.

10. Make sure you get your facts right.

11. Don't use **jargon** unless sending to the trade press.

12. Don't be afraid to send the press release by more than one method e.g. post, email, fax.

13. **Very important.** Follow up with a phone call asking if they need any further information, but don't hassle journalists.

14. **If they use your press release always say thank you.** Hardly anyone ever does and it will make them remember you. It's also polite!

If your story doesn't appear don't worry, it may have been bad timing. They could have had a lot of stories at that time – just keep trying!

Where to send your press release

In order to decide where to send your press release you need to decide what you are trying to publicise and who you want to reach. Your local paper may well be interested if you have won an award but wouldn't be interested in your new range of cards. A trade publication may be interested if you have designed a new range using unusual materials.

There are an enormous number of publications available in the UK today. A search on the internet will bring up a list of trade papers and a visit to a local newsagent will give you information about what is available locally. The media is generally divided into the following categories.

Local newspapers

This is a good place to start as they are always interested in local news and people and new businesses are often featured. They will want information about you as well as your business.

Trade press

There is a list of the trade press in the Fact File. Read them to find out the sort of story they feature and target with something similar. If you have a stand at a trade fair then you may get some publicity in the show edition of a newspaper.

Show organisers send information to all the trade press so make sure you supply them with images and pre-show publicity if you are asked.

Consumer/lifestyle magazines

There are a huge number of these on the shelves. Many of them rely on agencies to place products with them but some are anxious to feature the work of young designers. Spend some time researching these and compile a list of publications that feature similar products to yours. Don't forget that they have a long lead time and you will need to send Christmas card stories in August not November.

Local radio

There are a lot of radio stations around the country and many of them have talk shows which need a host of stories to keep them going. Identify some programmes that may be suitable, telephone the radio station, and ask for the name of the producer and contact them direct. If it is a current story then email or fax is quicker.

National press

It is very difficult to get into the national press but as even a small piece can give a huge boost you should keep trying.

The quiet times for stories, and a good time for you to try and get something in the paper, are January and August. Avoid clashing with national events such as Children in Need.

HOW TO GET PUBLICITY

Winning an award

If you win an award it can have definite advantages in gaining publicity. There are lots of awards around the country such as Young Entrepreneur, Livewire, Small Business of the Year, and Creative Businesses as well as the greeting card sector Henries.

A search on the internet will identify some awards, and keeping your eye on the local press will show you the ones in your locality. Keep an eye out for prize nights and you can put them in your diary for next year. You don't always have to win the award; being shortlisted or selected can be newsworthy.

Becoming an expert

If you become known as an expert on your product or business you can be called to speak at various occasions varying from local groups to business associations. These talks can be highlighted in the press, and when they need an opinion – such as an expert to say what they think about the charity card debate – they will call you, giving you even more publicity.

Seeing your name in print can become addictive. Always remember that the best PR translates into sales.

Using published information

If you are lucky enough to have a story published in the press then use it for extra publicity. Have the cutting blown up, laminated if suitable and use on your stand, send photocopies to all your stockists or your mailing list if trading through craft fairs. If you have several small pieces published then put them together on a piece of A4 and use this as a handout at fairs. People are always interested in this type of information and it will help you build your reputation.

It is a good idea to have a photograph of you taken for distribution to the press when required. It is worth paying to have a professional image with proper lighting taken when you are looking at your best, unless you have a good photographer in the family.

Example press release

Gay Quarter Cards

88 High Street, Manchesterford MN1 5XZ

2 February 200X

PRESS RELEASE

Launch of NEW Civil Partnership Cards

Jenny Smith and Christine Douglas are delighted to announce the launch of their new range of cards for Civil Partnerships. When they tried to organise their own Civil Partnership ceremony last year they couldn't find a range of cards which appealed to them, so decided to design their own to add to their range of traditional art cards.

Jenny said, 'The cards we found were mainly humorous or aimed at the male market; we wanted something more quirky yet stylish.'

The cards, which will be sold through high street retailers and over the web, have already attracted a lot of interest. **Kate Brown**, buyer at Celebrations Gift Shops, was very impressed with the cards. 'They fill a gap in the market and we are sure that they will prove very popular, particularly the invitations. The finish is very unusual and the colourful envelopes add style.'

Jenny and Chris will be exhibiting their new range at **Spring Fair 2008 Hall 4 Stand J1** and look forward to welcoming existing and new retailers to their stand. Their cards are also available on their website at **www.GayQCards. co.uk**.

The End

For further information contact Jenny Smith on 07801 xxxxxxxx

Card Sample & CD Image attached

13

Selling to retailers

It is possible to run a card business selling all the cards yourself through craft fairs and so on, or over the internet. Card companies such as MoonPig operate solely in this way, but the majority of businesses need to sell their cards through retailers if they are to grow the business. If you decide to sell to retailers – and it is very exciting to see your work on sale in shops – then there are a number of methods of getting your cards into shops.

Cold calling

One way is to visit the shops yourself. This is a good way to start off but is also time-consuming and therefore not cost effective, except during the early stages of the business and in your local area.

Trade fairs

Alternatively you can take a stand at a trade fair where retailers will visit you to see your ranges and hopefully place an order or enquiry. Exhibiting at trade fairs in covered in detail in Chapter 15.

Employing an agent

The third method is only viable when the business has grown to a certain size and that is to employ an agent. There is more information about this on page 141.

Other ways of supplying retailers

Sometimes you will find that a retailer at a craft fair who wants to stock your cards will approach you. (This is why it is important to have worked out wholesale and retail prices – see chapter 9.) Sometimes a retailer spots your cards in another shop and contacts you. Don't act surprised – you have a great product. Why shouldn't they want it?!

SELLING TO RETAILERS YOURSELF

When you are satisfied that you have a great range of cards which will be of interest to retailers, have worked out the pricing and are confident that you can produce them in sufficient quantity, then it is time to test the retail market. To do this first identify at least five card shops which might stock your work. Do your research by making sure that they sell cards similar to yours and at the same price points.

Approaching retailers direct

If you want to approach local retailers direct then do so in a professional manner. Don't walk in carrying a large bag of work and expect to be seen there and then. Call in, preferably during a quiet time, and with a letter, brochure, and/or CD of your range and a sample. Ask them if you can leave it for them to look at and make an appointment to come back and see them. If that's not possible at the time ring them in a few days and ask if they have had time to look at your work and then make an appointment.

◆ TIP ◆

If customers are in the shop always give them priority.

Mailshot

If you want to have retailers further afield stock your work then you need to do a mailshot. First identify the retailers you want to stock your cards; you can find a list of card shops at www.Yell.com or elsewhere on the internet. Unfortunately this won't tell you the sort of cards they stock so you will either have to ring them up and target specific shops, or do a blanket mailshot.

What to send

To do this, put together a package consisting of images of your work such as thumbnails or a brochure, a sample card and a covering letter. Send this to the shop by post.

Follow this up with a telephone call to gauge the level of interest. If you are trying to get your work into a new area then it is a good idea to plan a visit to the area; if retailers ask to see you then you know when and where you can visit them.

A selling pack

To be ready for visiting retailers put together a simple selling pack. This can be a couple of sample cards, a price list and a covering letter telling the retailer who you are and where you can be contacted. Always carry these with you in the car – you never know when an opportunity will arise to leave one with a potential retailer.

At an appointment

When you actually manage to talk to the retailer make sure that you have all your samples in good condition and in an easy-to-see format. A sheet of thumbnails is useful but they will probably want to see the cards themselves, and the packaging!

Be polite, know your facts but respect that the retailer knows their customers and what will sell for them. Listen to any advice such as 'We prefer cards with messages' or 'We can't sell abstract art'. Most retailers are friendly and will offer advice if asked, so learn from the experience.

◆ TIP ◆

Retailers complain that they are often shown really tatty samples, so make sure yours don't fall into this category.

Unless you have a professional brochure the retailer will prefer to see the full range of cards so always carry these with you in case you get an appointment straight away.

If the retailer says they are not interested try and find out why. If they don't think they can sell your cards try and find out the reason: is it the price or style? Take note of this, then move on, and don't take it personally. However if they say they are not taking any new ranges at the moment, ask them if there is any point in calling back after Christmas or later in the year.

Taking an order

Make sure you have an order form or a duplicate book in case the retailer decides to order. Know your options – if they ask if you can supply silver envelopes you should know if it is possible and if it will increase the price. Discuss delivery dates and make sure that they are realistic.

You can also discuss payment – some retailers will pay small businesses on delivery, others will expect you to supply them on sale or return until they know if your cards sell. Know what you are prepared to accept and stick to it.

Delivery

The most common complaint from retailers about small craft-based businesses is that they do not deliver on time. Make sure you agree an achievable date and deliver when promised with all the appropriate paperwork.

CRAFT FAIRS AND MAKERS' MARKETS

Many retailers visit craft fairs looking for something unusual, so remember to take your trade price list with you when you exhibit. This means that you don't have to discuss prices in front of your normal customers.

To increase your chances of this happening, write to all the retailers in the area (you can source their names and addresses over the web or *Yellow Pages*), send an image of your work and tell them where you will be exhibiting. If they don't attend the fair you can telephone them afterwards to see if they are interested in stocking your cards. The more proactive you are the better your chances of success.

TOP TIPS FOR SUPPLYING RETAILERS

1. Retailers like **exclusivity**: don't try and supply more than one retailer in a small town.

2. **Don't hassle** them. They know what they want to stock and what sells. Once you have got a firm 'no' accept it.

3. **Keep in touch** with retailers stocking your work. They like to know what you are doing, where you are exhibiting and so on. Either set up an email or postal newsletter.

4. **Provide point of sale** material and/or photographs or postcards they can use. An artist's statement is also useful, if appropriate.

5. **Be professional:** always deliver on time or let them know if you can't.

6. **Listen to what the retailer says** about your work. They are usually trying to be helpful, so if they say your prices are too high then think about it.

7. **If possible visit the retailer** before you contact them so that you know they are the right type of stockists. If you have just got their details out of the *Yellow Pages* then ring up and ask them if they stock your type of card.

8. Sometimes shops run out of stock **just before Christmas**. The large companies don't have spare stock nowadays so this might be a good time to try and get your cards into shops.

9. Always **leave or send samples**; a brochure or thumbnails are great but they will want to see the real thing.

10. **Don't expect the shop to set your prices** for you; you need to work out what you need to make a profit and how much you can realistically expect.

EMPLOYING AN AGENT

If you don't want to sell your cards yourself, or if you want to venture into different parts of the country, then you will probably need to employ agents. Agents are a good way of reaching areas of the country where you may not have any stockists, but they are expensive. You will need to be producing in quantity before an agent will consider taking you on as they depend on commission for their wages.

Agents are covered by European employment legislation, which means they are entitled to be treated properly and have certain legal rights. If you are employing agents then it is recommended that you seek legal advice in drawing up a contract. The agent themselves may supply one – in this case have it checked by your solicitor.

◆ TIP ◆

Remember that the agents only take the orders; you despatch the goods and are responsible for collecting payment.

Neither are they liable for bad debts although because they visit the retailers they should know who are reliable payers and which businesses may be in trouble. Agents will also want to be paid when the order has been despatched, not when you receive the money, so you need to allow for this in your cash flow.

Start with one agent

It is a good idea to start with one agent, possibly in a different area of the country to where you are situated. When you are confident that you can supply their orders then you can employ another agent.

Finding an agent

You can find agents by advertising on the noticeboards at the trade fairs or in greeting cards magazines. Alternatively, ask your local card shop to recommend an agent. If they don't cover the area you want they may know someone who does and a personal recommendation is useful. Taking on an agent is a responsibility but if you really want to grow your business then it will be essential at some point.

What to look for

◆ Good personality and appearance.

◆ Strong customer base within a given area.

◆ Similar products to yours but not too many.

◆ Check that the agent is familiar with the area he or she covers and preferably lives in the area. Time spent travelling is not spent selling.

◆ Ask how many times he or she actually calls on the outlets (five times a year is about average).

◆ Avoid agents who operate on the telephone once they have set the account up.

◆ Check how long they have been in business and avoid semi-retired agents. You want someone who is working for you, not treating it as a hobby.

Be prepared to interview potential agents as you would any member of staff. Take notes and construct a brief form so you have some record of what was discussed.

Communication

There is no point in employing agents if you don't keep them in touch with what is going on in the business: new developments, price changes and future plans.

As well as providing an agent with forms and paperwork for orders, it is a good idea also to provide them with a monthly report form so they can keep you in touch with what they are doing. You can reciprocate by sending them a monthly update. This is easy to do using email but remember that agents don't spend their lives in offices looking at computer screens so don't expect an immediate response.

◆ TIP ◆

Being an agent can be a lonely business and a regular phone call to discuss how things are going is often appreciated.

What the agent should expect from you

◆ To be given good product information, details about the company and to meet all the people they might come into contact with.

◆ To be given potential contacts quickly.

◆ To be kept in touch with price and design changes when they happen.

◆ **To be paid promptly**.

USING WHOLESALERS AND DISTRIBUTION COMPANIES

Apart from supplying the cards direct to the galleries there are two other methods of distribution. The first is wholesaling and the second is using a distribution company.

Wholesaler

Wholesalers buy the product from the publisher and sell it via their warehouse or using their own sales team. This method is unlikely to appeal to small card companies in this country but can be a useful way of entering foreign markets. In this case the wholesalers are often referred to as distributors. Using a wholesaler means that you lose some control over your business – you will have no say in who stocks your cards and it might be disappointing to find your upmarket cards on a market stall.

Distribution companies

In the UK there are a number of companies who will take on the distribution of cards for you. Their services vary so it is best to work out what you need and then find a company which offers these services. These services include:

- warehousing

- cello wrapping

- packing

- despatching

- sales administration

- credit control.

14

Craft fairs and markets

WHAT ARE CRAFT FAIRS?

Craft fairs are held all over the country each weekend and on bank holidays at a variety of venues. They can be a good way of starting to trade and gaining experience. They vary in quality and the type of customers they attract so try and visit several before booking a stand.

Popular venues

◆ stately homes

◆ village halls

◆ football stadiums

◆ shopping malls.

Sometimes they run alongside other events such as

◆ agricultural shows

◆ garden festivals

◆ boat festivals.

Craft fairs can be indoors or outside, but those that are outside tend to be held in marquees to ward off the British weather.

◆ TIP ◆

If you intend to do a lot of outdoor events which do not provide protection you will need to purchase a proper stand and gazebo to protect you against the weather.

In addition regular markets are held particularly in big cities such as Manchester and London where individuals are invited to take stalls to sell their handmade products. Sometimes these stalls are wooden structures and can be expensive to rent, reflecting the prestigious location.

Are they the right place to sell your work?

If you produce handmade cards then starting to sell them at craft fairs is generally a good idea. You can command a higher price than if you are selling them to shops and you will get feedback as to which designs will sell.

If you produce printed cards it is unlikely that these will sell well at a craft fair. Many artists sell cards at these events alongside their work. They are a good place to learn about selling and your skills, and you can also pick up a lot of information by talking to other stallholders and customers.

How do I find craft fairs?

If you have never been to a craft fair then visit as many potential venues as you can. Fairs are advertised as widely as possible in order to attract customers so you might find an advertisement in your local paper or in a specialist magazine such as *Craft & Design*. Alternatively you could visit one of the listing sites such as www.craft-fairs.co.uk, www.ukcraft fairs.com, or www.craftsman-magazine.com.

Art fairs and markets are listed in *AN* (Artists' Newsletter) and other artists' magazines. A search on the internet should provide you with a lot of opportunities.

> ◆ TIP ◆
>
> When you visit a fair ask the exhibitors whether they would exhibit at that fair again, if most of them say no then think twice before applying.

HOW DO I START?

Small local fairs will have lower fees and lower visitor numbers but they can be a good place to start. If you want to try one of the larger fairs then contact the organisers and ask for information. The big organisers usually have exhibitor packs. When you enquire you may be asked what type of craft you do – some fair organisers limit each type of craft to provide variety and you may have to join a waiting list. You might also be asked to supply samples of your work. This is to ensure that the exhibitors do make their own products and is a good indicator of the quality of the fair.

Which are the good fairs?

It is very difficult to know what type of fair is going to work for you. A fair that works one year may not work the next and this can be because it clashes with another event, or the weather is awful, or the publicity is not as good.

By visiting as many fairs as possible and talking to other stallholders you will start to build up a picture of a good craft fair. Beware of the ones that have a lot of bought-in goods or are badly organised. Many craft workers book the fairs in January for the coming year so you may find that good fairs do get booked up quickly.

How do I find a market?

Most markets are organised by the local council so the first step is to contact their markets' department and ask for a list of markets. If they don't organise them themselves they have to license them so will have a list of organisers. Covered stalls may be provided or not – do check as it can be quite expensive setting yourself up with a covered stall. Again, you may have to join a waiting list.

> **◆ KEY ◆**
>
> Be prepared – you may find yourself on several waiting lists. Make sure that if you get a telephone call only days in advance you are ready for the opportunity!

When you contact an organiser you could ask them the following:

◆ What type of people visit this fair?

◆ How widely is it advertised?

◆ Is the work contemporary or traditional?

◆ What are the stand fees?

◆ Are there any other costs involved, e.g. advertising, electricity?

◆ How are exhibitors selected?

◆ How many stalls are available?

◆ Is this an indoor or outdoor fair?

◆ If outdoors are there any provisions for bad weather?

◆ What is the average attendance?

Jurying process

Some fairs are juried i.e. the organisers insist on seeing the work prior to the event, and you can only sell the work they have approved. This means that the level of work on display is generally of good quality, so although it might be frustrating to have to go through the process it should pay off in the end.

Quota system

Some fair organisers operate a quota system that means that they only allow so many jewellers or card makers. This is to your advantage, but because card making is popular you may find it difficult to get into popular fairs at first.

Fairs v markets

There are some basic differences between fairs and markets. Customers will generally have to pay to get into a fair – this could be anything from £1 to £8. People who have paid £8 are not likely to worry about the cost of a card and will appreciate the work that has gone into them. They are often held in a venue such as a stately home or attached to an event such as a country show.

Markets, particularly in a town centre, can attract a lot of passing trade. These people may not understand the difference between your handmade cards and those that are mass produced so sales may not be as good. Only trial and error will tell you which market is right for you.

How much stock will you need?

The simplest answer is as much as you can produce. In the early days you will find it hard to know what is going to sell so the more choice you have the better, and if the cards sell well then you will constantly need to be replacing your stock. It's no use paying for a fair that lasts all day if you run out of stock at lunchtime. It looks very unprofessional.

Remember that seasonal variations will affect sales. Obviously in November you will have Christmas cards, but there is also Mother's Day,

Valentine's Day, Thank you teacher for the end of term, and a myriad of other occasions. Make the most of them. Some card makers find that Christmas cards sell all the year round, as people like to buy them in advance.

Designing a booth or stand

At a craft fair the design of your booth or stand and the display of your work are almost as important as the quality of the work.

◆ TIP ◆

Spend some time creating a good stand and you will find your work will sell better.

You may decide just to use the standard table for your first show but if you intend to exhibit regularly it really is worth having something purpose built. When you visit craft fairs you may see a stand that you like; you can then try and recreate it yourself or you can ask another craft worker to make it for you. Some craft workers do this as a regular part of their business. If you are making it yourself make sure that it is made of lightweight materials. You may have to carry everything quite a distance.

◆ TIP ◆

Don't forget to have a sign so people start to know your name.

Displaying your cards

You will need a good display if you are to attract customers and sell more than your competitors. An attractive display will draw people to your stand.

◆ Use professional card stands and spinners to display your work properly.

◆ Always cover the table with a cloth that reaches to the floor on all sides. It looks more professional and you can put all your other paraphernalia under it out of sight. Cover boxes to match to add extra interest.

◆ Use different levels to display the cards. It may be possible to have backboards with some cards on display.

◆ Practise your display at home; measure out the space you will have available so you know what to take and exactly how you are going to lay everything out.

◆ Know how much stock you have taken so you can work out what you have sold. If you are busy you won't have time to write down every sale.

AT THE FAIR

All craft fairs will allow you to set up in advance of the fair opening. Remember that you may have to park some way off and allow time to carry everything into the fair. Read the instructions for setting up carefully – you may have to access the site by vehicle between certain times.

Price everything so that it makes it easier for you and your customers. Shops always price their cards on the back to encourage customers to pick them up as this makes them more likely to buy. Keep pricing simple: it's not always easy to get change and it's a lot easier to add up cards at £2 and £3 than £1.98 and £2.76. Even so, you will need plenty of change. Everyone seems to tender a note even for a small sale.

◆ TIP ◆

Keep your money in a safe place. Always use a money belt to store your takings – you can't keep an eye on a tin. Unfortunately there are a lot of dishonest people around, even at craft fairs.

It is a good idea to have a clipboard handy to write any enquiries. For instance if someone wants wedding cards you can ask them to write down their name and address and get in touch later. You might also get an enquiry from a shop or gallery so make sure you know what your wholesale prices are and the type of quantities you can produce.

Try and have someone with you to help. This means that the stall is not left unstaffed when you go to the toilet or for your lunch – eating on the stand looks unprofessional. If there are two of you resist chatting to each other – this is very off-putting. Standing around all day can be very tiring so have a tall stool to perch on. It is better than a chair as it keeps you at eye level with the customer.

Making a sale

Smile and greet customers. A friendly word goes a long way and a stall with people at it, even if they are only looking, draws other people. If people are looking for a special card they may require assistance. It is possible to offer help without harassing someone so don't be afraid to talk to him or her, even if you start the conversation with a general question to help them relax. Some craft workers find this easier than others.

Have some paper bags ready to wrap the cards although many people nowadays will refuse them. A few plastic bags are also handy particularly if it's raining outside. Always thank people for the sale – they will remember that.

The reality of selling is that even though your work is good, you do everything right and the customer likes your cards, they will not always buy. Relax about losing sales at first; you will adopt a selling style that works for you and sales will increase.

Simple steps to help you make a sale

◆ When someone approaches your stand, stop what you are doing and concentrate on them.

◆ Greet all potential customers, smile and make eye contact.

◆ Ask them questions and *listen* to their answers

◆ If they seem interested tell them something about your work, what inspires your designs. Don't tell them how you do everything – everyone is allowed their trade secrets.

◆ Encourage them to buy by highlighting the features, e.g. unique design.

◆ If they are hesitating between two cards offer a small discount if they buy both.

◆ Say thank you.

◆ Ask for their details for your mailing list. Explain that you don't pass these on, it's just for you to keep in touch.

Leaflets

Even though craft fairs will be in different venues every month and attract different people you are trying to build a business and attract repeat custom, so it's also a good idea to have a leaflet ready to hand out. In addition to information about your cards this can have details of where they can contact you, other fairs you are going to attend, if you give talks and so on. If people like your cards they need to be able to find you again – the next time it might be 30 Christmas cards or wedding invitations. If you plan to sell over the internet you can include details of how to do this as well.

What to wear

This might not seem very important but you are part of your business and need to project the same image. Some craft workers have T-shirts with the name of the business printed on them. Alternatively you could have your card designs on the T-shirts and sell them as well.

There is no need to wear a suit but you should look smart and comfortable.

Don't forget your feet: you will be standing on them all day so comfortable shoes are a must.

AFTER THE FAIR

Pack everything away neatly and take your time – if you are in a rush you risk damaging stock. Leave your stand space clean and tidy. There may be instructions as to where you can leave rubbish, if not then take it home – you do want to be invited back. Evaluate the show, keep records of how much money you took and the number of people. You won't remember otherwise and it will help when booking shows for next year.

If this has been your first fair you may need to re-evaluate your prices. If you have completely sold out maybe you are selling too cheaply, if the fair has been busy and you haven't done very well then maybe you are too expensive for that venue. In the early days every fair is a learning experience. Hopefully you will have sold a lot of cards but if not you will have gained a lot of information.

15

Selling at trade fairs

One of the best ways to start selling to retailers is by exhibiting at a trade fair. These are held several times at year at different venues. Trade fairs are expensive, and exhibiting at the wrong fair can waste a lot of money. Before you book a show do your research: always try and visit a fair prior to exhibiting, talk to the exhibitors, look at the stands, and then send for an exhibitors' pack. The large trade fairs have waiting lists and may insist that you attend one of their smaller events before you are allowed into their premier show.

The following are the major shows in the UK for greeting cards.

◆ Spring Fair, Birmingham

◆ Top Drawer, London

◆ Autumn Fair, Birmingham

◆ Home and Gift, Harrogate

◆ British Craft Trade Fair, Harrogate

◆ Pulse, London

◆ Scottish International Trade Fair, Glasgow

New fairs are opening all the time and the format of existing shows is always changing, so check before you book.

Trade fairs offer a number of opportunities

◆ A chance to meet customers face to face.

◆ A direct way to launch new ranges.

◆ Opportunities for networking.

◆ A chance to review the competition.

◆ A place to source suppliers.

◆ A good place to find agents.

WHICH SHOW?

Trade shows vary in size and the market they serve. For instance, if you want to have your cards stocked by galleries and upmarket retailers then the British Craft Trade Fair in Harrogate or Top Drawer in London would be good fairs to consider. If you want to enter the mainstream card market and supply the large chains then the Spring Fair in Birmingham would be appropriate. This show is also good for export orders (see Fact File for details).

Most established exhibitions will be able to provide details of the number and type of visitors from previous events. This should give you a good indication of whether your type of customer will be there.

You can also check which companies exhibited at previous shows. If most of your competitors are there then maybe you should be too.

HOW TO APPLY

Contact the organisers and ask for an exhibitors' pack. First time exhibitors do not have a lot of influence with the show organisers so don't expect to get the best space the first time you exhibit. Some fairs have a waiting list or special entry requirements. Check carefully as to what you can exhibit and what is provided.

Many fairs can be booked up to a year in advance so you need to plan ahead. If you are travelling you will also need accommodation and this can be in short supply and expensive around the popular shows. Work out a budget and how many orders you will have to get to pay for the show. These orders won't all come directly at the show but if you find new customers who order regularly it will be worthwhile.

Before you apply work out a budget. Don't forget to include travelling and hotel costs, the cost of the stand and any publicity material. If you are employing people to help you on the stand you will also have to add in their wages.

◆ KEY ◆

All shows provide a show guide. Read this before you go as it will answer most of your questions and save a lot of valuable time.

YOUR STAND

When designing your stand make sure that it is eye catching, simple to erect and displays your product to the best advantage. Read the show handbook carefully and always mock up the stand at home; it's amazing how many newcomers arrive at a fair with twice as much furniture as will fit on the stand. Take note of the type of fixings you are allowed to use and remember to order lights.

For a trade show you need good quality samples well displayed. You also need a certain amount of stock, as people will expect to be given samples. You will not be allowed to sell off the stand so you do not need large supplies. Don't over-complicate the display, and show ranges together.

◆ TIP ◆

Don't crowd the stand. Make it eye-catching but not cluttered.

Don't forget

You will need a toolbox with the following:

◆ a selection of screwdrivers

◆ strong adhesive tape

◆ nylon thread or picture cord

◆ sticky tape

◆ craft knives

◆ tape measure

◆ extension leads

◆ light bulbs.

Many new exhibitors spend valuable time looking for the local DIY store when they should be setting up their stand.

BEFORE YOU GO

◆ **Don't forget to contact** existing and potential customers and invite them to your stand.

◆ If you have **people helping you** on the stand make sure that they know about the products and your business.

◆ **Allow plenty of time** to order and produce everything. If you are producing new ranges make sure the samples are ready well in advance.

◆ **Enter any competitions** that you are eligible for. This might mean that your cards will be on show in other places, which is very useful.

◆ **Prepare a press pack** to leave in the press office. Journalists looking for stories always visit this office and you never know who might see your cards.

◆ TIP ◆

Read the show guide before you go – again!

AT THE SHOW

◆ **Try not to eat on the stand** – it looks so unprofessional. Food is expensive at these shows so take your own sandwiches and make sure they are easy to eat discreetly if you are going to be unable to get away from your stand.

◆ **If you are on your own** then taking breaks and eating can be difficult, so make friends with the people on the stand next door and they can watch out for your customers.

◆ Always **leave your mobile number** with the people on the stand next door so they can ring you – you cannot afford to miss a potential customer.

◆ **Never sit reading newspapers** on your stand; if you find your business boring then so will your customers.

◆ **To stand or sit** is a dilemma. The professionals stand, but if it is your first show you might need to perch on a stool. This keeps you at eye level with the customer and prevents that terrible backache.

◆ **Your dress code should be smart.** This doesn't have to mean a suit – you could go for T-shirts with the company's logo – but being clean and presentable is essential. Comfortable shoes are a must, but not trainers.

◆ TIP ◆

Don't forget you will be on your feet all day and smiling!

Paperwork

Keeping track of the paperwork is not easy on a small stand, but if you lose a business card or potential customer's contact details you might lose a sale.

Always have the following on the stand:

◆ clipboard for attaching business cards

◆ price lists

◆ terms of trading

◆ product information

◆ order forms or order book

◆ pens

◆ mints.

◆ TIP ◆

Make sure that all the information you hand out has stand numbers on.

Dealing with customers

Have a clipboard ready for keeping track of customers' names and addresses. If they haven't got a business card then just give them the clipboard to write on.

> ◆ TIP ◆
>
> Never give out any information or samples to people whose name and addresses you don't know: they could be competitors trying to copy your cards.

Smile at everyone, and have a series of opening lines. It is a well-known fact at trade shows that stands that look busy attract more people; buyers will look twice if they think someone else is interested. Spend time talking to people even if they are only saying, we love your cards but we own a pet shop.

If you are going to limit the number of shops which stock your cards in each town – and many retailers will ask for exclusivity – then make sure you have details of current customers to hand. Accepting an order and then having to turn it down is not good practice.

> ◆ TIP ◆
>
> Know your production levels. Don't promise if you can't deliver.

Promoting

You will need business cards and leaflets to promote your business; these can be handed out on the stand and left in the press office with a press release.

Catalogues/brochures

Some card companies produce catalogues, but the industry is very fast moving and designs change quickly. Many companies send their agents out with samples rather than brochures.

You can easily produce a catalogue on your computer featuring your designs and it is a good idea to have one of these available to give to the retailer even if you also carry samples. If you have a large number of ranges and a small stand you can have a brochure available on a laptop for them to look at, as well as the actual cards.

Trade show special offers

Some exhibitors offer special deals for people ordering at trade shows. For instance it could be if you buy £300 worth of cards you receive a free spinner. This can be a good way of trying to get your work into shops. Or you could have a sample pack of six each of 20 designs for £100. Whatever you do, make sure that you are not losing money.

AFTER THE SHOW

Create a database with all the contacts you have received. Send a thank you for visiting the stand, and if they have ordered send details of when their order will be despatched. If they haven't ordered you can send them more information as a reminder or arrange for an agent to call.

Most importantly, despatch the orders when you said you would. This is the biggest complaint retailers make – that small suppliers don't deliver on time. If you have a crisis and can't deliver then let the customers know. If you have agreed to let them have credit then check out their references.

Keeping in touch

It is important that you keep in touch with retailers and tell them of any development. Everyone likes to be associated with success, so if anything special has happened – perhaps you have won an award, been chosen to design a card for Prince Charles or taken a large order from America – then send them a newsletter (see Chapter 18 for more information on networking).

BUILDING A BRAND

In recent years people have started to develop a loyalty to a card brand particularly at the top end of the market. Having people ask for your cards is the best way to promote your business, so having a clear image and building a brand can be very effective.

What makes a successful brand?

Successful branding is about promoting your strengths – in the case of a small business that is you. What are you good at? What do you believe in?

For example:

◆ Excellence in design

◆ High-quality customer service

◆ Providing good value for money.

If you want to build your brand and feel that your cards have all the qualities indicated above then you need to try and get your name in front of the public. You can do this by promoting yourself (see Chapter 12 on PR), by entering for awards such as The Henries (organised by Progressive Greetings), and also local business awards such as Start-up Business of the Year which are generally advertised in your local paper. Supplying your retailers with point-of-sale material also helps to reinforce your name to customers.

16

Alternative ways of selling

Whilst craft fairs or selling to retailers will continue to provide the main source of income for most card businesses, finding other ways to sell your cards not only spreads the risk but also means that you have a more regular income.

The growth in the amount of retailing carried out on the internet is amazing but because cards are generally of low value the card industry has not really profited from this growing sector. There are, however, ways in which you can make it work for your business.

There are several different methods that you can use to sell your cards. The main ones are:

◆ selling by party plan

◆ renting shelf space

◆ selling over the internet

◆ the wedding market.

In order to find out if any of these methods are right for you, look carefully at your cards, who buys them and where they shop. This may seem like a simple question but it is in fact the crux of your business. The customer is the person who makes the business; try staying in business without anyone buying your products – how long will you last?

Growing with your customers

Your card range can also grow with your customers. For example if you are targeting the student market you can decide to stay with that, or you can decide to move with them when they begin to settle down and start families. Their tastes and needs will change and you could then start to produce wedding invitations or children's cards.

SELLING BY PARTY PLAN

The image of selling by party plan has improved since its first associations with plastic kitchenware. It is now one of the most successful methods of direct marketing and can be used to good advantage by card makers. It has many benefits including a captive audience, occupying a short period of time, having low overheads and the need to carry less stock. It can also provide customer feedback for those card makers who generally supply shops and galleries and do not deal directly with the customer.

> ◆ TIP ◆
>
> If you are not skilled at selling then it is possible to find someone to run the parties.

It helps if the range of products on sale is varied, so it might be a good idea to team up with, perhaps, a jeweller or sell other products to keep it interesting.

If you are to keep people entertained for a couple of hours you may need to consider combining your work with other craft workers in order to provide variety. You could try organising a quiz with questions about cards such as how many years is a silver wedding anniversary? If you give a small prize it can help people enjoy themselves.

How to get started

As with any business you need to plan ahead. Work out the level of commission you can afford and prepare some printed price lists and order forms.

Where to hold a party

Most people begin by holding a party in their own, or a friend's, home. Organisations and charities also run these events in halls and other venues. You should aim to book at least one party at each event to ensure continuity.

What to sell

In addition to selling individual cards, try boxing or packaging cards together to maximise sales. Some card makers also do well by selling card-making materials alongside their cards. People will often buy a kit to have a go and then realise how difficult it is – so it won't affect sales in the long run!

Incentives

You will need to work out how much you can afford to give the hostess for holding the party, but it is generally between 10 to 20 per cent in the value of goods. Charities want cash so you will need to take this into account. Some party planners give everyone a free small gift, a gift card or something similar and others find that playing a game with a small prize helps to break the ice.

Finance

The general feeling is that people will spend more if they order on the night and pay later. Ask everyone to fill in an order form – the hostess will need a copy of these if she is to collect the money. If people want the card quickly they will want to buy on the night. Alternatively they might want to commission something special like a personalised card.

Arrange the delivery date at the party and arrange for the hostess to have the money – do not leave goods unpaid for. If you cannot deliver the item ring the customer and ask if they will accept an alternative. Always keep a note of all customers' names and addresses as they will form the basis of your mailing list.

Remember – for a successful party

◆ Make it entertaining – it is a social occasion.

◆ Offer incentives for booking parties.

◆ Include a re-order form with all orders.

◆ Keep a list of all customers and use for mailshots.

◆ Avoid school holidays.

◆ Parties work well in the run up to Christmas.

RENTING SHELF SPACE

An option which is becoming increasingly available and popular is that of renting shelf space in craft galleries, tourist attractions and shops.

How it works

You pay the owner to rent a space where you display your cards, and they are responsible for selling your goods and for the upkeep and maintenance of the selling space.

Market research

The same principles apply as to craft fairs: you need to do your research thoroughly to find out the sort of goods that sell best there, the type of visitors the place attracts, how well the outlet is maintained and the throughput of visitors at different times of the year.

This type of selling works best during the busy pre-Christmas season, and during the tourist season in tourist areas, but you will probably have to sign a contract to exhibit during the quieter times as well.

Evaluating the potential

Before embarking on this type of venture try and talk to other people who are already there. Go there as a visitor and send your friends. Find out how easy it is to purchase the goods – are the assistants reading books or do they make a genuine effort to help customers? You need to know if they are familiar with handmade products, can they answer questions? Also, do the owners advertise widely; are there special promotions; will you have the chance to demonstrate?

Advantages of this type of selling

This can be a good solution if you want to test the demand in another area.

It can also work well if your goods are closely related to the venue, e.g. a range of wildlife cards at a bird sanctuary.

They can be useful for selling off stock which hasn't sold to shops as an alternative to attending a craft fair.

Remember

◆ Don't just put your goods in there and forget about them. Check the display regularly and top up sold stock.

◆ Find out who is responsible for items that are broken or shoplifted.

◆ Ask if they will take orders and pass on commissions.

◆ Ask how regularly they pay; ask other renters if their system is efficient.

◆ How did you find out about the space – will other people find it easily?

◆ Are your price points compatible with theirs?

◆ KEY ◆

The results you get from marketing your work are usually directly related to the amount of time and effort that you put in.

THE INTERNET

The growth in sales of all types of consumer goods over the internet during the past two years has been huge. Unfortunately this opportunity has not helped the card industry. Because the unit sale of a card is so low and the cost of running a commercial website very high you need a large turnover to sustain a commercial site, and most consumers seem to prefer buying their cards from shops.

However there are businesses that use the internet effectively. Hallmark is one of the larger companies whose site offers free Ecards but also sells flowers and gifts. Smaller businesses have a lot of advertising on their site, which obviously helps to cover the costs of running an expensive site.

> ◆ TIP ◆
>
> Although Ebay is not a great way to sell cards it is very useful for sourcing suppliers.

Do you need a website?

Because it is difficult to sell cards over the internet you may wonder if it is worth having a website. The answer is definitely yes, your customers need to be able to find you and the internet is the perfect way for them to do this.

Domain name

As soon as you decide to set up in business you need to choose a name for your business. In today's trading arena you need to find something that you can also register as your domain name. To do this choose a name and check on one of the sites such as www.easyspace.com to see if your name is in use. If it's an unusual name you might be lucky, if not you might consider spelling it differently or choosing something else.

When you have decided upon your name register it so no one else can use it. Do this even if you are not in a position to set up a website yet. You can always have a page set up which says 'website under construction' and gives contact telephone numbers or an email address. As soon as you can, convert this into a website so that people will know you are trading.

What to sell over the internet

If you are hoping to build up a business in a specialist market such as wedding stationery, where the value of the sale is likely to be high, then an internet site may prove very lucrative. It is also good if you take commissions for specialist cards such as embroidered christening cards.

How to take orders

If you decide to trade over the internet then you need to decide how you are going to take orders. There are several methods if you want your customers to pay over the internet. PayPal, or a similar system, is the obvious choice as it provides you and them with security. Ask your website designer to work out the cost of this and if you think it is viable ask them to set it up.

When you are just testing the market, or want to start in a small way, you can have an order form on the site for people to print off. They can then fill it in and send it off with a cheque. If you take credit cards then they could ring you up and you could take payment over the phone. Don't forget to add postage.

10 top tips for marketing your website

1. Decide what you are going to use your website for – information, building a reputation, selling etc. This will affect the way you promote the site.

2. Write the copy as you would an advertisement – don't leave it to the web designer.

3. Promote your website on everything: van, shop windows, letterhead, business cards, T-shirts etc, and don't forget to put your website on your emails.

4. If you are selling through the website then have some business card/postcards specially printed and distribute as widely as possible.

5. Link to as many other websites as you can – it's free and effective. www.webring.com provides a free navigational tool that links 'rings' of sites based on common interest.

6. Manage your website on a regular basis or pay someone to do it for you.

7. Use the website to collect information on potential customers. Include a feedback form, ask them for information, or offer something free. This will give you their email address.

8. Sign up to the Google adwords site. You pay only if people click on your ads – www.adwords.google.com.

9. Learn about keywords and how they affect your positioning on the search engines.

10. Advertise your website in publications. Even a small lineage advert in an appropriate publication can have dramatic results.

♦ TIP ♦

Reply promptly to all enquiries. Just because you can't see your customers doesn't mean they aren't still there!

THE WEDDING BUSINESS

Weddings are huge business in the UK, and fortunately for card businesses the sector is not price sensitive. When you consider that the average cost of a wedding is £15,000, to spend £500 on invitations is nothing. Themed weddings are also popular and this opens up a number of opportunities for small card businesses, as the cards supplied by the large companies tend to be fairly standard.

♦ TIP ♦

Weddings get cancelled so don't forget to take a large deposit.

In addition to invitations you may be asked to provide some of the following.

♦ orders of service

◆ place names

◆ menus

◆ thank you cards.

This can add up to a substantial order. You might need to print inners on the computer or you can ask a printer to do this and then attach them to the inside of the card.

How to target the wedding market

Exhibiting at wedding fairs

Virtually every bride-to-be visits at least one wedding fair, so it makes sense to advertise your cards at these. The best ones are very expensive, so see if you can join forces with a photographer or wedding cake maker and have a joint stand to cut costs. You will need fliers or a brochure to hand out; you can also leave these at wedding venues and with other wedding suppliers.

Advertising in magazines

There are a lot of bridal magazines on the market, and many brides buy them all. You don't need to advertise in them all, but you do need to make your advertisement stand out and also try and get some editorial at the same time (see Chapter 12 on PR).

Personal recommendation

Weddings tend to run in age groups – many people attending a wedding will also be getting married themselves so put your name and contact details on the back of the card. This can be done discreetly but it's amazing how many small card designers don't bother.

Civil partnership cards

There has been a recent growth in the demand for civil partnership cards. If you intend to target this market you could advertise in gay magazines or leave your fliers in gay bars.

There are now wedding planners who specialise in civil partnerships; a search on the web should give you some contact details. As with wedding cards, word of mouth is a great way of marketing and once you have successfully been commissioned for one partnership you will probably find other people asking for quotes.

17

Selling skills

When asked to list the skills you need to run your business effectively you probably answer: maker, designer, accountant, driver and so on. You probably won't list salesman/woman, or if you do you don't give it a very high priority. However if you don't sell anything you won't remain in business very long. Selling is a crucial part of running a business and yet we rarely give it the priority it deserves.

Why don't we like to think of ourselves as salesmen/women? Is it mainly because they have such a bad image? But there is a world of difference between a double glazing salesman trying to hit targets and a maker selling their product to a customer by describing how it was made, where his inspiration came from and so on.

SELLING OPPORTUNITIES

To be successful you need to take advantage of every selling opportunity that comes your way. If you are proud of what you produce then you should have no problem selling it to other people. Presumably you are offering value for money, and they need a card, so what's the problem?

And yet for many people there does appear to be a problem. To sell your own products you need to come to terms with two things:

1. Don't take rejection personally. Not everyone is going to like your cards.

2. If you don't sell anything you won't be able to keep making, and that would be a shame.

PROPER PREPARATION

Whatever you are selling, good preparation, customer focus and effective interaction with the customer will all help you to make the sale.

Some people are naturally gregarious – they talk to people about their work and are happy to do so. They think they are selling but in actual fact although they are communicating very effectively, they are not making sales.

Do some research

Salespeople are everywhere, although their techniques are of varying quality. Next time you go to buy something, watch the salesperson at work. Look at how they interact with customers, what their sales techniques are – are they pushy or professional, or do they look bored and as if they don't care?

Next time you make a purchase, decide what made you buy that particular product. If the salesperson helped how did they do it? Did the product live up to the salesperson's promise? Did they find out what you wanted or did they try and sell you something that was on special offer?

10 RULES FOR SUCCESSFUL SELLING

1. Make a good first impression

It is very important when you are on your stand at a show that you look professional; it is just as important when you are approaching a retailer or holding a party. Stand holders who sit eating their lunch or reading the newspaper are a definite turn-off for customers. You don't need to wear a smart suit or designer clothes but you do need to look clean and tidy. If you are visiting a potential outlet don't have a baby under your arm; you are running a business and you want someone to buy your cards so be professional.

2. Build your confidence

If you really lack confidence in this area try building it by listening to tapes or CDs, or reading a book, about super confidence. The bookshops are full of them, or your local library might have one you can borrow. Look on it as learning a new skill, just as if you needed to learn bookkeeping. Practise selling regularly on friends or family and ask people for constructive criticism.

You could go on a sales course but they can be expensive. Instead read a book about selling and practise some of the techniques. If you lack experience go and do some voluntary work in the local charity shop – it will help you get to grips with selling and when it's a good cause you might find it easier.

3. Effective communication

Clients sometimes tell me that they cannot talk to a stranger, yet they can ask someone when the next bus is due or for directions. It's a matter of having a purpose and you have a purpose – to make a sale. Start a general conversation with a potential customer to discuss your work, ask questions to find out what the customer is interested in and needs. Don't stand there talking about the weather, how difficult it was to find the shop, and the state of the parking. This is chit-chat not effective communication and it won't make you a sale, even if the customer goes away thinking what a nice person you are.

4. Ask the right questions

There are basically two types of questions you can use when you are selling: open questions and closed questions.

Closed questions invite a monosyllabic response: 'Can I help you?' 'No.'

Open questions can start a conversation: 'How can I help you?' 'What type of card are you looking for?'

Always use open questions as these will lead to a conversation and give you the opportunity to get to know more about the customer. Give information to start a conversation, for example 'The design on those cards is created using special metallic powders.' Once you get a customer talking you can begin to find out what they like and show them the sort of work they want to see.

5. Develop listening skills

Being listened to properly is very flattering and it is something that in today's hurly-burly world often gets forgotten. If you miss something the customer says or don't understand, ask them to repeat it. Don't interrupt a customer. This can be difficult if there is another prospective purchaser near by and the person you are dealing with is probably a time waster, but how you treat them will be seen by the potential customer. Say something positive like, 'Do you think we could continue this conversation later after I have helped this lady?' and gradually move away.

6. Use the customer's language

Don't be a smart alec; you might know what every technique is and the posh name, but if your customer thinks it's a lovely card then that's what it is. If you are listening properly you will have honed in on the customer's level of knowledge and be talking to them at the right level. Be aware that some customers might also be card makers and don't give too much information away.

7. Sell the benefits not the features

Benefits are 'sending a handmade card will make someone feel really special' or 'it's something that your friend can keep'. Features are 'every card is handmade', or 'the cards are made from recycled paper'. You can give them this information but always remember that it is how the product will impact on their lives which is important.

8. Set targets

Whatever you are trying to sell, and wherever you are doing it, set targets. When you attend any selling event have an idea in mind of the amount of money or orders you expect to take. Keep this in the forefront of your mind. Set rewards, for example if we hit our target we will go out for a meal tonight. Be realistic and don't set unachievable targets; base your forecast on what you did last year or last week. Don't only set financial targets – you could aim to get 20 customers onto your mailing list.

9. Price points

Try and find out how much your customer wants to spend. It is very difficult to judge level of income; the lady in the designer clothes may be an astute shopper who buys from charity shops, and the old lady in the ancient designer coat with a piece of string for a belt might own half of Lincolnshire. Treat them all the same and when you find out what they intend to spend guide them to goods at that price point.

10. Take away

Make sure the customer goes away with something such as a flier or a business card to remind them of you. They can always order from your website or send you a cheque.

And finally: keep positive

People who sell for a living know that they get nine rejections before making a sale, and every time they get a rejection they celebrate as it means they are closer to their goal. This is not easy to do but if you can master it then it will help you increase sales.

THE ELEVATOR PITCH

The elevator pitch is an American selling technique. The idea is that if you meet a potential contact or customer in a lift you should be able to tell them about you and about your business before the lift arrives at their floor.

Example: you find yourself in a lift with the buyer for cards at John Lewis. You have 30 seconds to try and get them interested in your cards.

You say, 'Hi, my name is Elizabeth White. I am the owner of Think Cards, a handmade card company specialising in upmarket cards. We believe that we are making a big impression in the marketplace. I think my cards would sell well for you. Can I send you some information/come and show you the cards?' Hopefully the answer is yes – you can then give them your card or ask for theirs. Follow this up with the information reminding them where you met.

SELLING TO PROFESSIONAL BUYERS

Professional buyers are just that: professionals. They use different techniques and are generally very good at negotiating good deals and getting what they want. They often use silence to intimidate inexperienced salespeople so beware – don't try and fill every silence. Wait for them to answer you (repeat a rhyme in your head if you find it difficult to keep quiet).

They will almost certainly try and get a discount; know exactly how low you can go and what quantities you can deliver and when.

> ◆ TIP ◆
>
> Don't be afraid to walk away if it's not a good deal for you. No business can afford to run at a loss no matter how much you want to see your cards in their shops.

CUSTOMER CARE

When you find customers look after them. If it's a new retailer then ring them after they have received their first order; ask them if they are satisfied and how the cards are going. Hopefully nothing will have gone wrong but if it has then you must be in a position to sort it out quickly so resentment doesn't build up and you lose a customer.

When you have been trading a while then why not carry out a customer survey, either in person, by post, email or telephone? This can be quite brief but you might pick up some useful information. Everyone likes to be asked for their opinion.

Customer survey

For a craft fair simply have sheets of paper with four to six questions on a clipboard and ask everyone who makes a purchase or is a known customer to fill it in. If you are a newcomer you can use it as a way to collect names and addresses – even offer to put it in a draw with a prize if you think people will be reluctant to take part.

Try the following questions:

1. What items have you bought from us in the last 12 months?

2. Why did you buy them?

3. Were you happy with the service we provided?

4. What else could we have done to make the product/service better?

5. Will you buy from us again?

6. If not, why not?

Internet customers

Don't forget your internet customers. Ask questions like

1. Which product did you purchase?

2. Why did you buy it?

3. Was the buying process easy?

4. How did you find the website?

5. How could we make the process better?

Retailers

If you only supply retailers, treat them as customers and ask them similar questions. Good retailers will give you feedback, but you do need to ask. In their case a telephone survey may be most successful. Phone at a quiet time and ask them:

1. Are you happy with the quality of the cards?

2. Are you happy with the delivery time?

3. Are you happy with the point of sale material?

4. Have any customers made any useful comments about the cards?

5. What could we do to improve the service?

It may seem simple, but just asking customers what they think makes them feel important and the amount of information you can gain from even a short survey can help enormously to build your business.

18

Networking

Networking is an important part of any business. Many people are put off by the idea yet it is simply about going to places that attract your kind of customers, and talking to people who can help you with your business. You then have a chance to meet them, explain your business and find a way to keep in touch.

Networking also gives you the opportunity to meet other people in business to share valuable tips and information, take workshops, and gain access to much-needed business services.

TYPES OF NETWORKS

◆ business groups

◆ social groups

◆ specialist groups

◆ women's networks

◆ informal networking

Business groups

Every town has a number of networking groups for business people; the Chamber of Commerce or organisations such as the Federation of Small Businesses may organise them. If you join one of these organisations they often have meetings for new members, which makes it easier to join in.

There are also specialist networking groups which have regular breakfast meetings. These often demand quite a commitment from their members and set targets for gaining new business. Some people love them, others hate them.

♦ TIP ♦

The Greeting Card Association is the main business organisation for the industry. Even if you can't go to meetings, joining it will give you access to a wealth of information and help.

Social groups

Social groups, such as golf clubs, can also be good for networking. You could also join other organisations such as the friends of the local art gallery or round table. Any organisation which brings you into contact with people can be useful.

Specialist groups

If you want to exhibit at craft fairs it may be worth joining your local craft guild. They often organise fairs and are very supportive so should be able to help in lots of ways.

Women's networks

Women often find it more difficult to network than men and are intimidated by male-dominated networking events. Because of this many women-only network groups have sprung up. If you are a woman and nervous about networking they are an excellent place to start, but if you are serious about building up a business then you will have to talk to men as well.

Informal networking

In reality everywhere is a networking opportunity. You could even start a conversation about your business in the queue at the supermarket. Maybe you won't sell any cards but you might find the member of staff you were looking for.

When you have attended a couple of meetings you may decide that an organisation is not for you – in that case move on. Don't waste time; there are plenty of opportunities out there. Networking is just talking about your business and making contacts who can help you grow. If you were enthusiastic about golf you would probably join a golf club, so presuming you are enthusiastic about your business then why not join a networking group?

ATTENDING AN EVENT

Preparation

If you are nervous about networking, prepare a few questions before you go so you are ready when you meet someone new. Virtually everyone is nervous when they attend their first networking meeting.

At networking events

◆ People expect to exchange business cards.

◆ They are all looking for contacts as well as you.

◆ Choose a network that is good for you – some of them are very proactive and set each other targets.

◆ Avoid networks that are full of accountants and solicitors.

◆ It's better to go alone so you don't get stuck talking to the same person all the time.

Do your homework: try and find out who will be there and make a point of meeting people who may be particularly useful. You should always try and network upwards – networking is a two-way process and there will be people there who want your help which is fine, but your purpose is to make contact with the people who can help you.

Joining a group

When you walk into a networking session spend a few minutes surveying the room, and try and pick out a group you could join. For instance avoid groups of two people who are having an animated conversation. Look for a gap in a group of three or more, walk up, smile, and wait for them to increase the circle. If there is a silence introduce yourself, they will then do likewise. Don't be embarrassed if someone leaves the group; they may have just been waiting for the opportunity and you have provided it.

Moving around the room

When you have introduced yourself to the people in that group and possibly exchanged cards, it's time to move on. If you are stuck in a group of two with probably the most boring person in the room then you could suggest that you both go and join another group. This is easier than abandoning someone. You can then leave them with that group and move on yourself.

TOP NETWORKING TIPS

◆ Arrive early at events so you can look at the guest list.

◆ Networking needs a clear head, so stick to soft drinks.

◆ Every person you tell about your business could tell 10 other people.

◆ Don't offer your card outright. Wait for them to ask for yours or ask them for theirs – then you can exchange cards.

◆ Make notes about the person on the back of the card. It will make it easier to sort them out if you collect a lot of cards.

◆ Everyone you meet is a potential salesperson for your business.

◆ Keep your business cards easily accessible in your pocket – a lot easier than at the bottom of your handbag.

Keeping in touch

Follow up the people you have met and add them to your database. If you have promised to do something or send some information then do it.

NEWSLETTERS

Newsletters can be a very effective means of communication, providing a link between yourself and your customers. They can be used to advertise your presence at shows, to launch new products or to remind customers of your range. Newsletters are relatively inexpensive to produce and can be distributed via your mailing list, given to customers at craft fairs and included with orders.

What to include

Your customers, whether wholesale or retail, will generally be interested in any developments you make in your product range and it is often easier for them to assimilate the information through a newsletter rather than just a price list.

Include personal information if you enjoy having a social relationship with your customers. Many of them become friends over the years and do like to keep in touch. Some of the best newsletters involve the customers in the business by sharing details that they wouldn't have otherwise known.

Producing a newsletter

Producing a newsletter couldn't be simpler. The advent of personal computers and desktop publishing packages has made it easy for people to produce newsletters professionally at low cost. Photocopying is widely available at very reasonable prices. If possible use slightly heavier paper quality than is usually available, it does make a difference and costs very little extra.

Use illustrations where possible. If your computer skills won't allow you to draw then consider some of the images available on graphics packages and find someone who can scan one in. If all else fails paste the illustration on after you have written the newsletter and before photocopying.

Newsletters are most effective if produced on a regular basis. Every three months is a good interval unless you have something special to announce. You can include special offers, discount vouchers or even carry advertising for fellow craft workers to help with the cost.

If you find it difficult to think of something to write about, think of the type of questions you are asked at craft fairs or when you visit retailers. This is the type of information that is most likely to appeal to your readers. Details of commissions, exhibitions, awards won or the use of new materials are all of interest to your customers.

BUILDING A DATABASE

You need to start keeping a database of customers as soon as you start trading, whether this is potential retailers or customers at craft fairs. Every contact you make is valuable. If you keep the names on a computer you may need to register under the Data Protection Act – see www.ico.gov.com.

Mailing out regularly allows you to keep in touch with your customers and build brand loyalty. They will probably expect a Christmas card – after all you are a card company – but don't forget the special occasions of other groups such as Jewish New Year, Eid and St Patrick's Day if they feature on your database.

19

The environment

All businesses today have to consider the impact they make on the environment. Whether this is to do with recycling, using sustainable products or maximising use of resources depends on the type of business. As the greeting cards industry uses a lot of paper it is natural that concerns are expressed about the impact of this on the environment. Currently the greeting cards industry is not a major focus of environmental groups but it is advisable to be aware of what is happening.

What about the cost?

The slight increase in price that using recycled products involves does not seem to have an effect on sales where companies have introduced it. In fact many customers now actively seek out products which have good environmental credentials.

A greater impact on the environment which card manufactures may need to consider is the manufacturing of cards in China with the consequential increase in carbon footprint as they are transported around the globe. Producing locally not only helps local industry but also saves the planet.

AREAS OF CONCERN

The main areas of concern for the industry are:

◆ board

◆ envelopes

◆ cello wrap

◆ surplus stock

◆ consumables

◆ transport.

BOARD

Recycled board used to be more expensive than ordinary board, and this was the reason given by many businesses for not using it. However recently prices have equalised. As this situation continues to improve it is likely that recycled card will form the basis of the card industry in the near future. One problem some card companies have is finding a recycled board that is 'white' enough. Recently, however, this problem also seems to have improved.

ENVELOPES

There are few arguments against using recycled envelopes. Consumers would be unlikely to notice the difference and the costs are now similar.

◆ KEY ◆

If you want to take this subject further you can apply to be a member of the FSC (Forest Stewardship Council).

CELLO WRAP

The biggest problem for the card industry is the cello wrap, which is difficult to recycle. Recent innovations include wrapping cards in bags made from cornstarch which is compostible; it is however slightly more expensive. With the current emphasis on recycling and concerns about the environment hopefully it won't be long before someone develops a biodegradable cello bag.

SURPLUS STOCK

Another major concern is the greeting card mountain. Because of the savings made when cards are printed in large quantity, when cards don't sell there can be a huge quantity to be disposed of. In recent years card shops selling old stock have opened up in outlets and shopping centres to try and sell off these cards. There has been a mixed response to these shops – some people believe they hit mainstream sales, others see them as broadening the market.

Even the most environmentally aware businesses struggle with the problem of surplus stock. At the very least they can be recycled.

Used cards

Disposing of used cards is the responsibility of the consumer. With local recycling schemes now becoming more widespread this should be less of a problem. Major retailers such as Boots and Tesco offer recycling schemes for Christmas cards which help solve one of the major problems.

CONSUMABLES

Not only do environmental problems belong to the product, there are also concerns about the use of computers, electricity and other consumables. In any business today you need to be aware of the resources you are using and whether there is a better way – for instance obtaining your electricity from an environmentally friendly source.

TRANSPORT

Making the most efficient use of transport is in everyone's interests. If you use a carrier to transport your cards you might want to ask them about their environmental policy, as well as being concerned about your own transport arrangements.

LABELLING

Currently there are no regulations governing what information needs to be printed on the card (such as how much recycled material has been used), but this may come with time.

Defra (Department for Environment, Food and Rural Affairs) set guidelines for correct labelling. They suggest the following:

◆ You should make it clear whether the claim refers to the card, the envelope or both.

◆ It should refer to a specific forest certification scheme e.g. FSC, PEFC.

◆ You should comply with rules set by the particular certification scheme regarding use of the logo, the working of the claim and the 'chain of custody' requirements. To use specific logos you should contact the scheme involved and obtain permission.

◆ If the scheme allows a percentage then state the percentage content of the source.

Terms which are best avoided

Sustainably managed forests – there is no approved definition of this.

Carefully managed is also meaningless.

Renewable – again, no widely accepted definition.

One tree planted for every tree cut down – as most of the card and paper used in the industry comes from commercial forests this is normal.

Checking with your suppliers

You need to check when purchasing supplies if they fit into any of the schemes. Get proof in writing before stating it on your cards or you could have problems.

How important is it?

When setting up a small business there is so much to think about that the above might not seem to matter, but as you grow it becomes a bigger issue. If you start out doing this properly it will be easier to operate in a larger market.

One of the largest greeting cards companies, Hallmark, has a member of staff whose sole purpose is to make sure that the company is as ethologically ethical as possible.

Examples of an environmental management system

◆ All waste cardboard compressed into bales for mill recycling.

◆ All polythene, plastics and shrink film segregated and sent for specialist recycling.

◆ Staff attend environmental awareness seminars.

◆ Damaged and returned cards recycled.

◆ All envelopes made from recycled paper.

◆ Monitoring of transport to ensure effective use of resources.

You may already do most of the above. If so it is important to let your customers know – it might improve sales.

20

Copyright and licensing

PROTECTING YOUR COPYRIGHT

Copying is rife in the card industry and as soon as your cards start appearing on the shop shelves you are vulnerable. Someone else who has more money and more outlets can copy your work and produce ranges which are very similar. There are two schools of thought as to how you should tackle this.

1. Stay ahead of the game

Some manufacturers believe that as the card market is so fast moving by the time someone else has copied you, you have already moved on. Although it is very annoying to have someone else steal your designs, the best way forward is to stay ahead of the game.

2. Protect your work

The other viewpoint is that you should protect your work at all costs and fight every case.

The right course of action is probably somewhere between the two. Firstly you should do all you can to protect your work and take legal advice if you are copied, but be wary of pursuing action through the courts as it could cost you a lot of money.

> **◆ TIP ◆**
>
> It is not only large firms who infringe copyright. Many small manufacturers copy designs so be careful who you show your work to.

Are you at risk?

However you sell your cards – at craft fairs or using agents – if you are producing your own cards you run the risk of them being copied once they are out in the marketplace. To protect yourself it is a good idea to investigate joining an organisation to protect yourself against this happening.

How to protect yourself

There are various organisations that offer copyright protection. The main ones are ACID (Anti-copying in design) and Copywatch – the Gift Associations scheme. Alternatively you could take out an insurance policy to protect yourself. Several firms of lawyers specialising in intellectual property rights operate these schemes (see Fact File).

You can also help yourself if you

◆ Adopt an effective and efficient document and management system. Do this by keeping signed and dated records of all initial designs – ask a friend or colleague to sign or witness them. The design process may well involve several stages so make sure they are each recorded.

◆ Keep photographic records.

◆ Either use the date function on the camera or email them to yourself.

◆ Design register products before you put them on display at a trade ow. The Registers Community Design came into effect from 1 April

2003. Designers need make only one application, which costs approximately 320 euros, which covers the whole of Europe for up to 25 years. The more designs you register the cheaper it is.

◆ You may want to consider the life of your product before registering and whether it will be easy for someone to change it slightly and create a new design. Registering a new design at OHIM (www.oami. europa.eu) at the UK patent office (www.patent.gov.uk) can take up to three months. If you prefer to rely on unregistered UK design rights (basically the only protection you have is a record of your work – very difficult to prove in law) then consider using one of the design registers who store your designs for you. When you register them an acknowledgement is sent providing vital evidence at a future date.

◆ Always use the copyright symbol on your product and if registered give the design register and the number.

◆ Keep records of where and when the designs first went on sale.

◆ At a trade fair beware of people with cameras or sketch pads. Always call security if you think you are being copied.

◆ Don't forget that it is possible for two people to have the same idea particularly if it is fashionable or reflects a current event. Before you start registering designs check to make sure no one else is producing the same or similar designs.

◆ TIP ◆

Don't be guilty of copying
If you are using someone else's design remember to check that they are their designs and that they are in a position to sell them to you.

Following any meeting with potential customers always confirm what happened in writing, saying who you saw and what you showed them.

Always state:

'All intellectual property rights in our designs are and will remain the property of (your business name). Any infringement of these rights will be pursued rigorously.'

If you belong to one of the protection agencies then include their logo.

Include this clause in your trading terms and conditions and display the logo on all correspondence and publicity material and your website.

If you are at a trade fair and find you are being copied don't tackle the copier straight off. Try and get proof – obtain copies of their catalogue or other information. Send other people, preferably a buyer, to see the stand and maybe even get samples. If you belong to one of the anti-copying organisations visit their stand and ask for help.

◆ TIP ◆

Threatening to thump someone, however satisfying, is not going to help your case in the long term!

Nor is becoming despondent. Try and work out the reasons they have copied your work and why their copies are selling. Obviously the main reason is because the designs are great, but usually they will have altered them slightly – maybe made them more contemporary. If this is the case and you find their cards are selling better than yours then look at your design skills. Have you been so busy running a business that you have not kept pace with the market? Being copied is an unpleasant experience but it can also be a good opportunity.

REGISTERING A TRADEMARK

Trademarks are signs, symbols, logos, words, sounds or music (such as jingles) that distinguish your products and services from those of your competitors. A trademark can be one of the most powerful marketing tools you have; it can help people recognise the quality and design of your product.

A trademark must be distinctive for the goods and services you use it for. Providing you can represent your trademark in words and pictures you can register it in the UK. Registering it establishes in law that it is your trademark and belongs to you alone. You then have an automatic right to sue anybody who infringes it. In fact just registering it can serve as a deterrent to people who might otherwise infringe it.

How to register

To register you need to apply to the UK Intellectual Property Office (UK-IPO). The forms and details of the fees payable are on their website www.uk-ipo.com.

LICENSING

What is licensing?

Licensing is a way of allowing other people to use your designs or images (your 'intellectual property') on their products, while you keep control of the copyright. A licence is a legal agreement which allows the owner of the property (the licensor) to grant a manufacturer or retailer (the licensee) the right to use the property on specific products usually in a defined area over a defined time period.

To use an image that is covered by copyright – including cartoon characters – a card maker must pay a licence fee to reprint that image in their own designs. The fee differs depending on the type of image used and the amount of times it is reprinted.

◆ TIP ◆

New card designers are often offered a fixed fee rather than a licence. If your cards sell well you may be able to negotiate a licence next time.

How do I get paid?

The licensor generally pays a guaranteed fee and/or a royalty on a percentage of the sales of the product. This is negotiable but when you are first starting out you will generally have to accept the fees offered by the licensee.

What are the advantages of licensing?

◆ It allows you to enter new markets which would be difficult on your own.

◆ It generates new revenue streams.

◆ It builds your image.

◆ It can provide a good extra income with minimum work.

How does it work?

A licensing agreement covers four basic areas:

◆ Product – this will indicate the type of products on which the design can be used e.g. greeting cards, mugs, T-shirts etc.

◆ Term – the length of time the licence contract lasts (after which the rights revert back to the artist/owner of the copyright). The normal length of a licence is two years.

◆ Territory – this will state the country or countries to which this licence applies.

♦ Royalties – royalties are paid as a percentage of the trade price. These vary from 4 to 12 per cent depending on the quantity and value of the product. Royalty rates for well-known artists and television characters can rise to 15 per cent.

How much will I be paid?

You can negotiate the fee yourself or use an agent who negotiates deals with print and card publishers. Good licensing agents should be able to negotiate better terms and have a wider range of contacts than individual artists, even allowing for the commission. However some publishing companies will only deal with artists direct. Licensing agents typically charge their artists a commission in the region of 30 per cent. A typical fee is £150 to £200 an image. Standard commission is 15 per cent going up towards 20 per cent.

Licensing charity cards

The selling of charity cards by card companies is very popular. It is mutually beneficial to both parties both in increased sales and building a brand. The arrangement is a legal one covered by the Charities Act 1998, which states that the contribution to the charity is not a donation but a payment for the use of its brand name and logo.

Despite the adverse publicity that sometimes occurs in the press, charities are very grateful for the income generated by the sale of cards in this way and do their best to build up a good working relationship with card companies involved.

How to set up a royalty agreement with a charity

♦ Decide which charity you wish to support. If you are a small company this could be a local hospice or other local charity; the large charities are unlikely to be interested unless you are going to have substantial sales.

- Contact the charity with your proposal – number of designs, quantities involved and the commission per pack.

- Charities generally accept that a commission of 10 per cent (excluding VAT) of the retail price is a reasonable return and one accepted by the public. This can be divided amongst several charities.

- If the commission level is too low the result can be bad publicity for the card producer, the charity and the retailer.

- Many of the larger charities have their own royalty agreement but if they don't you will need to have one drawn up by a solicitor.

- The card designs need to be shown to the charity for their approval. Check that none of the images may offend the charities' donors e.g. people smoking on a card for a cancer charity.

- If necessary ask to see the charity's mission statement.

- All artwork that includes the charity's 'brand', e.g. the name logo and website, must be approved by the charity. Most charities are very keen on maintaining specific colours.

- The charity's registration number must be printed on all artwork.

- The contribution statement (i.e. how much the charity is going to receive) must meet the requirements of the Charities Act 1998. It is advisable to check wording and format with the charity at every stage as mistakes can be expensive and it is your responsibility.

- The contribution statement must be printed either in the brochure (business to business) or on the card pack/box (retail) and on the relevant website page.

- Payment is generally made to the charity's trading company because it will incur VAT.

◆ KEY ◆

It is the responsibility of the card company to meet the requirements of the Charities Act and it can be fined heavily if it fails to do so.

Showing designs to large firms

There are many ways of showing your designs to potential buyers, such as visiting their stands at the trade shows or contacting them via their website. Before you hand over your originals, do some checks. Try and find out the names of the other artists they represent and talk to them. Ask them for their experience – some card companies insist that artists change their designs so much that the artist no longer feels that the work belongs to them. Also try and find out if they have made any money. If you have to keep reworking designs that initial fee may soon seem paltry.

There are no standard licensing agreements. Most companies have their own and, particularly for new designers, these are non-negotiable. If you have a really unusual idea and are concerned about it being copied you can ask the company to sign a letter of confidentiality – some will, others won't – and then you have to assess the level of risk.

Resources

◆ LIMA – the Licensing Merchandisers' Association. Tel 020 7082 0802 www.licensing.org.

◆ Licensing Pages, www.licensingpages.com, is a business resource which provides members with information on all aspects of licensing as well as providing a range of special commercial tools to aid day-to-day activities.

◆ *The Licensing Source Book* is a useful source of information about the licensing industry. Tel 020 7700 6740, www.max-publishing.co.uk.

- Federation Against Copyright Theft, www.fact-uk.org.uk.

- The Copyright Licensing Agency, www.cla.co.uk.

- Copyright registration, www.copyrightservice.co.uk.

- www.ideas21.co.uk.

- www.acid.uk.com.

- www.ga-uk.org/our_services/copywatch.

Technical terms

Board	Paper becomes board when it weighs over 170 gms.
Calendered	Smooth or polished paper.
Caliper	Thickness of a single sheet, expressed in microns.
Embossed	Paper which is pressed on engraved steel rollers to create the desired effect.
Felt marked textured	To resemble felt.
Laid	Vertical and horizontal lines which can be seen when the paper is held up to the light.
Laminated	Board is sandwiched between self-adhesive film, matt or gloss.
Pearlised	Paper that has had a pearl coating applied, usually to one side.
Rigidity	The force required to bend either paper or board.
Varnishing	A thick layer covering the entire board, applied during Litho printing.
Spot varnish	As above, but applied only in specific areas. Both are available in matt or gloss.
Coated board	Coated board usually provides a sharper image, or one with a punch finish – not suitable for all designs.

Uncoated board	Although there is a huge selection of uncoated boards, they are used when a tactile finish is important.

SOME USEFUL PRINTING TERMS

Artwork	This can be original drawings or computer generated work.
Back-up artwork	This is printed on the reverse side of the sheet.
Bleed	The design is printed larger than the finished card so it may be trimmed and therefore not leave a white border.
CMYK	This is a four-colour process using the colours cyan, magenta, yellow and black.
Hexachrome	As above but with the addition of purple and orange inks.
Colour Bar	A bar printed during the colour process to check density and quality of the inks.
Diecutting	The cutting out of shapes using a special knife.
EPS	Encapsulated postscript file: a standard computer file used for graphics and text.
Finished	The processes applied when the job has been printed. Can include folding, stapling, diecutting, embossing.
GSM/GM2	Grams per square metre: a measurement to calculate the weight of paper.

Pantone	A universal colour-matching code system to ensure continuity.
Litho	The most common method of printing greeting cards.
PDF	Portable document file: a universal file that can be opened on most systems.
Proof	A sample of the card for you to look at to check the details. Once the proof is approved it will be printed.
Registration marks	When printing more than one colour these marks must be aligned to achieve a perfect image.
Reprographics	The transfer of data from photographs or images into a format ready to print.
RIP	Raster image processor: a computer system, either hardware or software, which converts digital files into the necessary dots ready to print.
Separation	The process where colour images are separated into individual colours.
Tiff	Tagged image file format: this is a dot format computer file, mainly used for photographs.

Fact File

UK TRADE FAIRS

British Craft Trade Fair (BCTF)

The main trade show for crafts and design-led goods in the UK.

When	April
Where	Yorkshire Showground, Harrogate
Contact	PSM
	Tel. 01273 833 884
Website	www.bctf.co.uk

Craft Hobby and Stitch International

When	February
Where	National Exhibition Centre, Birmingham
Contact	ICHF
	Tel. 01425 272711
Website	www.ichf.co.uk

Design Edge

When	September
Where	Sandown Park Exhibition Centre, Sandown, Surrey
Contact	PSM
	Tel. 01273 833884
Website	www.bctf.co.uk

Home and Gift

A show which is very popular with northern buyers. It has a good section for small card producers.

When	July
Where	The Exhibition Centre, Harrogate
Contact	Clarion Retail
	Tel. 0207 370 8843
Website	www.clarionretail.co.uk

The Museum & Heritage Show

For those whose products are suited to this market.

When	May
Where	Earls Court Exhibition Centre, London
Contact	Every Events
	Tel. 01905 724734
Website	www.museumsandheritage.com

Select British

Strongly supported by buyers in the south west.

When	June
Where	Westpoint Exhibition Centre, Exeter
Contact	Select British
	Tel. 01934 733433
Website	www.selectbritish.co.uk

Scottish International Trade Fair (SITF)

The show inevitably has a Scottish flavour and attracts a lot of international buyers. A second show is held in the Autumn.

When	January
Where	SECC Glasgow
Contact	Clarion Retail
	Tel. 0207 370 8843
Website	www.clarionretail.co.uk

Spring Fair (ISF) and Autumn Fair

The Spring Fair is one of the largest fairs in Europe, and most of the major card companies exhibit. To exhibit here is very expensive – good options are to join a group stand such as Focal Point or Design Gap.

When	Spring: February
	Autumn: September
Where	National Exhibition Centre, Birmingham
Contact	emap TPS
	Tel. 0207 8277 5800
Website	www.springfair.com

Top Drawer Pulse

These shows are primarily for design-led gifts, fashion accessories and jewellery. They attract a lot of overseas buyers.

When	Spring: January
	Pulse: June
	Autumn: September
Where	Earls Court Exhibition Centre, London
Contact	Clarion Retail
	Tel. 0207 370 8843
Website	www.clarionretail.co.uk

Torquay Fair

One of a small number of regional fairs, this one serves the south west and is a good exhibition for those whose work supplies the tourist market.

When	January
Where	Riviera International Centre, Torquay
Contact	Hale Events
	Tel. 01803 206302
Website	www.ercb.co.uk

Wales Spring Fair

Running alongside a gift fair, this is primarily for those producing in Wales.

When	January
Where	North Wales Conference Centre, Llandudno
Contact	Wales Craft Council
	Tel. 01938 555313
Website	www.welshcraftscouncill.co.uk

INTERNATIONAL FAIRS

There are a huge number of international fairs. It can be useful to look at what is happening in other countries – check out their websites and combine it with a holiday.

New York International Gift Fair

This fair has a large section of craftworkers.

When	January
Website	www.nyigf.com

National Stationery Show

Where   New York
Website   www.nationalstationeryshow.com

Ambiente Frankfurt

The fair to visit in Europe for anyone interested in design.

When   February 2007
Website   www.uk.ambiente.messefranfurt.com

Showcase, Dublin

Has a large number of exhibitors sponsored by the Crafts Council of
Ireland and is good for small card companies.

When   January 2007
Website   www.showcaseireland.com

SUPPLIERS

Board merchants

Fedrigoni UK
18 Queensbridge
Old Bedford Road,
Rushmills
Northampton NN4 7BF
Tel 0845 0714408
www.Fedrigoni.co.uk

GF Smith
Lockwood Street,
Hull HU2 OHL
Tel 01482 323503
www.gfsmith.com

Premier Paper Group
Tel 0870 2250171
www.paper.co.uk

Envelope suppliers

Caledonian Envelopes
Dryburgh House,
Meikle Road,
Livingston EH54 7DE
Tel 01506 498300
www.caledonian-envelopes.com

The Envelope Printing Co.
Unic C
Centurion Way,
Erith,
Kent DA18 4AF
Tel 020 83335353
www.envelope-printing.co.uk

Cello-wrap Envelopes

World of Envelopes
Madison Commercial Ltd.
Unit A2
Knaves Beech Industrial Estate
Loudwater
Bucks HP10 9Qy
Tel 01628 8100
www.worldofenvelopes.com

Card stand suppliers

5eh
Teale Group
Kirklands Workshop,
43 Drummond Street,
Mulhill
Scotland PH5 2EN
Tel 01764 684878
www.5eh.co.uk

Luminati
Unit One,
Redlake Industrial Estate
Bittaford,
Ivybridge,
Devon PL21 0EZ
Tel 01752 698700
www.luminati.co.uk

Card suppliers

Graphicus Ltd
Fountain's Court,
High Etherley,
Bishop Auckland
DL14 0LZ
Tel 01388 834934
www.graphicus.co.uk

Craft Creations
Ingersoll House
Delamere Road,
Cheshunt
Hertfordshire
EN8 9HD
Tel 01992 781900
www.craftcreations.com

Kookykards
Sadlers Hall Farm
London Road,
Basildon
Essex SS13 2HD
Tel 01268 569420
www.kookykards.co.uk

Publications – Trade

Progressive Greetings
Max Publishing
United House
North Road
London N7 9PD
Tel 020 77006740
www.progressivegreetings.co.uk

Greetings Today
Lima Publishing
Naishville
1 Churchgates
The Wilderness
Berkhamstead
Herts HP4 2UB
Tel 01442 289930

Publications – Consumer

Complete Cardmaking
Practical Publishing International Limited
Europa House,
Adlington park,
Macclesfield,
Cheshire
SK10 4NP
Tel 0870 242 7038
www.practicalpublishing.co.uk

Cardmaking & Papercraft
Beautiful Cards
Quick Cards Made Easy
Origin Publishing Ltd
14th Floor
Tower House
Fairfax Street
Bristol BS1 3DN
Tel 0117 927 9009

Index